RESTORATIVE JUSTICE

RESTORATIVE JUSTICE

Prison as Hell

or a

Chance for Redemption?

JENNIFER FURIO

Algora Publishing
New York

ISBN: 1-892941-74-0 (softcover)
ISBN: 1-892941-75-9 (hardcover)

Library of Congress Card Number: 2002013146

Jennifer Furio.
Restorative justice / Jennifer Furio
    p. cm.
ISBN   1-892941-74-0 (softcover)
          1-892941-75-9 (hardcover)
Restorative justice. Victims of crimes. Criminals—Rehabilitation. Corrections—
Philosophy. Criminal justice, Administration of—United States.
Includes bibliographical references.
HV8688 .F87 2002
364.6/8 21
                         2002013146

Front Cover: Drawing by Veronica Compton, State Penitentiary, 1985

Printed in the United States

Table of Contents

"Oh, Man, what doth the Lord require of thee, but to do justly and to love and walk humbly with thy God?" Micah 6:8

FOREWORD

It's time to get tough on crime! How often do we hear that refrain from our political leaders? A colleague of mine had an interesting way of challenging this view. "If we choose to live by an 'eye for an eye' and a 'tooth for a tooth' philosophy, we'll soon have a whole bunch of one-eyed toothless people walking around!" he said.

Although this is an overstatement to many, a person need not look far to see many graphics effects of the way we "do" justice. The United States now imprisons more adults than any other industrialized country. Driven by a view that punishing offenders will deter crime and make communities safer, governments and justice officials continue to support expansion of one key industry — prisons — sending more and more men and women to jail, and for longer periods. Yet, despite the lack of any credible evidence to show that this punitive view of justice is providing safer communities and reducing crime, our justice system marches on, based on an assumption that we simply need more and more of the punishing same.

But how is this justice system serving us? Are jails rehabilitating and healing offenders? Are victims being heard, compensated and helped? Do local community members feel any sense of involvement and empowerment in the system? Perhaps it is the assumptions underlying a system based on retribution that need to be challenged. Perhaps it is time to consider involving offenders, victims and community members in a new process of justice. And perhaps it is a time to listen to new and enlightened voices in the justice debate.

Jennifer Furio is one such voice. As the author of three published books dealing with various aspects of crime and punishment, Jennifer now turns her attention to the emerging and challenging world of restorative justice. Showing the variety of applications for restorative processes, her work considers new ways that offenders, victims and local community members can become involved and empowered within the criminal justice system.

As a lawyer, and author, working widely in the Canadian criminal justice system, I fully recognize the need for offenders to take personal responsibility for their actions. But there is also a need for society to consider the damaging effects of our current strategy. In our clamor to "protect the public," I believe we have lost sight of the human faces of people in our courts and our jails — those we have labeled as "criminals." And I so doing, I believe we have also lost sight of the views and needs of victims.

I spoke at a restorative justice meeting last year at a local church. One woman there described how she had recently visited a women's prison. There she had met many inmates, all native Canadians, all in their early twenties, and all mothers of young children. She was moved by the comment of another visitor to the jail: "They were all somebody's baby, once." The soul of a little girl, now within the body of young woman, and now separated from the outside world by a set of bars, provided a very different picture of how we are trying to protect our community.

One question rarely considered by those who support a "get tough" view on crime is whether justice has an existence outside the physical elements — such as police, courts and jails — and outside the prevailing "just deserts" philosophy which drives our system. In this book, Jennifer

Furio considers, as one application of restorative philosophy, the work of Chuck Colson, former assistant to President Nixon. Colson's work in founding and expanding Prison Fellowship ministries makes clear what I believe to be the unavoidable truth — there is a connection between spirituality and justice.

Before Christmas, I was involved in court case in a rural Saskatchewan community. It involved a prolonged and violent fight at a drinking party at a local native community. Eighteen men were charged in this melee. Almost all had been charged in this altercation, yet most were also victims of assault during the fight. One man had almost died of his injuries, after being airlifted to hospital. At the sentencing of all offenders — which followed a series of restorative healing circles between offenders and victims — this man told the assembled circle what this incident and restorative process had meant to his life, previously characterized mainly by alcohol abuse. By sparing him, this man said he believed God had given him, and his family, a second chance.

I felt the spirit blow through the courtroom that day. And I believe that the stories, insights and testimonials presented by Jennifer Furio in this book bring that spirit to us, through new ways of looking at justice, and new opportunities for involving offenders, victims and community members in a justice system previously dominated by professionals. We see these opportunities in the chance of restoring torn relationships, and in the hope that offenders and victims will in some way find a healing presence emerging from their anger and grief. And we feel the hope of new pathways to justice when we question the wisdom of existing justice practices, especially as our society jails young women — someone's baby, just a few short years ago — who now look at the faces of their infant children through pictures.

There are no easy answers to the multitude of questions posed about the justice system. Many voices are heard everyday suggesting a variety of approaches. Hopefully, this informative book will serve as a way of interesting many people in an alternate view, called restorative justice.

Ross Gordon Green, Q.C., c. 2002

INTRODUCTION

When I undertook to do a sociological study of criminals in 1996, the question in my heart, as I addressed these faceless and destructive people, was, "What right do you have to harm others?" It never dawned on me that I would come to know these criminals as human beings, that I would begin to understand their perspective, that they too were victimized. And so a vicious cycle began in my own mind: I felt guilty for feeling bad for them as well as for the victims — for everyone involved. After all, wasn't I studying criminals in order to help serve victims? In the end, I realized that the only way to stop the perpetual cycle of violence was to accept the offender on a very different level than I'd ever believed I could. A level of grace was demanded of me — a demand to sit and listen to a criminal's history, because until I had done that, I really couldn't understand "why."

Once the process of allowing all the voices in, of gathering all the information from every side, began, my assessments changed entirely. My perspective on our justice system shifted, and I became concerned that if there was not a systematic change in the way we think, socially and judicially, we were looking at global failure — not just community breakdown.

I relied on my own faith to help me understand why I was not hating. My negative and dismissive judgments were dissipating. Was I losing my perspective? Was I losing my mind? Was I siding with evil? The truth is, the more I delved into the study of criminal behavior, and into victimization, I found it impossible to reach in and grab hate from any region of this "prison" of horror: places we don't see when we are sitting in our college classes, or our pleasant homes nestling in quiet neighborhoods.

Behind closed doors, in so many homes, the cycle begins — without our seeing it. The mother hits the baby, the father hits the mother, and both get drunk and have sex in the room where the six year old is hiding, trying to watch television and tune out his fear. He is terrified. And so it goes . . . and so he grows. And so does the rage from watching such scenes repeat themselves day after day. Then, in his own rage, after a few bottles of beer a few years later, he decides his girlfriend deserves a good whack across the face. Maybe if he uses his beer bottle, she'll really get the message. His mother always did.

Restorative justice is an innovative approach that is based on a profound appreciation of the miracle that is the human being: a miracle of ongoing creation. In the pages that follow, we will take a look at some of the structures that can make restorative justice a success for people with a criminal past who desire to create a more promising self for the future. It is an approach that makes sense, and the time has come to apply it more widely.

WHAT IS RESTORATIVE JUSTICE?

Restorative justice is an innovative movement within the field of criminal justice. Restorative justice programs are based on ethics, on the conviction that all persons deserve to be treated with some semblance of decency. Facing the stare of a cold-blooded killer, it can be hard to stand by that belief; unfortunately, we can only get past the ugliness of the current situation by looking closely at specific alternatives.

The concept is broad, and naturally branches out to encompass issues of personal and community relationships — considering that, like any other population, any other collective unit, our criminal facilities are filled with interaction, conflict, and the need for resolving conflict. In essence, this (relatively) new approach aims to apply the principles of restorative justice as a response to offenses and crimes throughout a community.

Restorative justice is not a trick to "give prisoners a break." It may sound dreadfully liberal — "Free the prisoners" — but that is not the goal. Rather, it is an effort to provide a solution to violence and ultimately to bias and conflict. In fact, it has to do with restoring the soul, the humanity of the criminal, even if parole from jail is not a possibility.

The rationale behind restorative justice is not to let prisoners off easy. Instead, it is to offer an alternative perspective to our definitions of punishment and of the criminal himself.

Different methods of dealing with criminals have been tried in different ages and different cultures throughout history. In a sense, efforts to "restore" criminals have been the norm in Europe for decades, but the United States has taken up the concept seriously only in recent years. It has finally become policy, in many locations.

In 1982, the Victim Offender Reconciliation Program (VORP)[1] was founded at California State University, Fresno. It was the first such program in California and has served as a model for use throughout the country, even the world. Restorative justice as an ideology evolved into judicial policy in part from the work of Ron Claassen and the VORP. The Community Justice Conference was first to recognize that to provide an offender the opportunity to "restore," that is, to return to the fold, to reinstate himself as a member of the society that he had offended, might indeed be more effective than repeated or long-term incarceration.

By 1995, the United Nations NGO Working Party on Restorative Justice adopted the principles of restorative justice as a foundation for global prison environments.[2] In many communities in the United States, county courts, probation departments, and district and public attorneys, in collaboration with VORP, have developed pilot restorative justice programs. The Community Justice Conference transfers substantial sentencing authority to the communities in non-violent felony and serious misdemeanor juvenile cases and even, when possible, in crimes such as rape and/or murder. In this book, we will examine specific communities and illustrate how the members of a community can work together to alter what might appear to be hopeless circumstances —

---

1. A wide range of articles describing this program, which was spearheaded by Ron Claassen, are available at ‹http://www.fresno.edu/pacs/docs/›.
2. "Leading Edge," *Jubilee Magazine*, 1996, John Braithwaite.

circumstances that provide no answers to a victim, and no solutions for an offender.

While the basic framework is to systematically change the way people treat each other, we have to think about demographics before we can determine the most successful approach. Is the community large or small, urban, isolated, less-educated, higher-income? These attributes help tell us what resources, what institutions, what attitudes might exist; what we have to work with, and what we have to work around. Once this has been taken into account, the community leaders and stakeholders can meet formally and informally to debate, discuss, refine and implement restorative justice principles. We can find a catalyst for change, a map for the future, and a centralizing force in changing the face of the world, one community at a time. But how?

Specific principles have been established and must be adhered to in accordance with criminology and restorative justice. The vision is a radical and positive change in human relations — even between an offender and his (or her) victim.

Restorative justice can be described simply as a specific strategy, road map or set of guiding principles. The concept must be respected, for it works not only at higher judicial or larger global levels than the general public may realize but, just as important, the blueprint can be adjusted to accommodate "A – Z" levels of criminology, all aspects of criminology.

Restorative justice follows a clear process, in fact, a "blue print." While the program must remain flexible, depending on the circumstance, one blue print or another (at a very high maintenance level, for example, or at a less-demanding level) is necessary.

Here is part of the framework[3] that the Fresno County Restorative Justice program utilizes (© 2001, California State University, Fresno):

---

3. 2002. Ron Claassen et al. "A Blueprint for Restorative Justice" in *Services of the Restorative Justice Project of FPU* [online]. Fresno, CA: Fresno Pacific University, June 2000 [cited July 2002]. Available at ‹ http://www.fresno.edu/pacs/docs/rjframe0201.pdf›.

1. Leaders must decide to introduce restorative justice within their organizations, agencies, workgroups, congregations, schools or homes.
2. Stakeholders analyze how restorative justice principles relate to conflicts, disputes and offenses affecting them. They bring in outside assistance, if necessary.
3. Stakeholders evaluate and discuss current processes for responding to conflicts, offenses, and misbehaviors.
4. Stakeholders examine how others have used restorative justice principles to guide their programs. (This is a key element, as these principles are core to Restorative Justice as a methodology and as a movement.)
5. Stakeholders design and develop, with outside assistance if needed, a plan for organizational change based on restorative justice principles.
6. Stakeholders implement restorative justice principles, using both their own trainers and outside trainers.
7. Stakeholders evaluate their progress towards systemic change based on restorative justice principles.
8. Restorative justice principles should guide organizational change.

In the following chapter, the fundamental importance of "principles" is examined.

Principles of Restorative Justice

Successful implementation of this approach relies on a framework. Still, while the principles provide an outline, the programs view crime in an alternative light and perceive each circumstance as deserving of its own punishment and healing. By the same token, the governing of restorative justice requires that the communities recognize that each must maintain an open attitude, expanding or contracting on particulars as appropriate. This is the framework that was developed for Fresno, California:

1. Restorative justice is a way of thinking, and responding to conflicts, disputes or offenses. Restorative justice concerns making things as right as possible for all people.
2. Restorative justice recognizes that response to conflicts, disputes or offenses is important. Restorative justice responds in ways that build safe and healthy communities.
3. Restorative justice is not permissive. Restorative justice prefers to deal cooperatively and constructively with conflicts, disputes and offenses at the earliest possible time and before they escalate.

4. Restorative justice recognizes that violations of rules and laws are also indicators of transgressions and offenses against persons, relationships and community.

5. Restorative justice addresses the harms and needs created by, and related to, conflicts, disputes and offenses.

6. Restorative justice holds disputants and offenders accountable to recognize harm, and repair damages as much as possible. It creates a civil future.

7. Restorative justice empowers victims, disputants, offenders and their communities to assume central roles in recognizing harm, repairing damages, and creating a safe and civil future.

8. Restorative justice repairs the breach and reintegrates the victim, disputant, offender and their community as much as possible.

9. Restorative justice prefers maximum use of voluntary and cooperative response options and minimum use of force and coercion.

10. Restorative justice authorities provide oversight, assistance and coercive backup when individuals are not cooperative.

11. Restorative justice is measured by its outcomes, not just its intentions. Do victims emerge from the restorative justice response feeling respected and safe? Are participants motivated and empowered to live constructive and civil lives? Are they living in the community in a way that demonstrates an acceptable balance of freedom and responsibility? Are responses by authorities, community and individuals respectful, reasonable and restorative for everyone?

12. Restorative justice recognizes and encourages the role of community organizations, including the education and faith communities, in teaching and establishing the moral and ethical standards that build up the community.

The discipline systems in American schools, by the way, look and operate in ways that are similar to the US criminal justice system. Experiments based on the above principles have shown promising results, demonstrating that much of what is being learned in terms of improving the effectiveness of our approach to criminal justice might also be applicable within the school system. In light of the growing violence at schools across America, this is important and bears further work.

Steve Gonzalez, principal of a Minnesota high school, reported in 1996 that "in the year following limited attempts to put into practice the Principles of Discipline that Restores, formal home suspensions dropped by 31%, and referrals to the principal dropped substantially. The safety and general overall environment also improved."[4]

While the primary focus of the current study is prisons, our schools provide a useful environment for parallel studies. Conflict is ever-present, and the (for the most part) smaller population allows for deliberate interaction between theory and practice that could be examined thoroughly.

---

4. At the conference of Peacemaking and Resolution, Minneapolis, MN.

MEASURING RESULTS IN RESTORATIVE JUSTICE

Restorative justice is becoming much more than an ideology, a high-minded idea that remains to be proven. Early programs have been in place long enough to show convincing results. In fact, in several states (and countries worldwide), there are employees within the department of corrections who have been designated to provide education and promote Restorative Justice.

Numerous models for measuring results were presented during a conference on Restorative Justice recently sponsored by the US Department of Justice. The DOJ has established several research projects in an attempt to explore the reasons for success of some models and programs in the growing field of Restorative Justice.

Ron Claassen, who is currently Co-Director of the Center for Peacemaking and Conflict Studies at Fresno Pacific College, developed what he calls the J-Scale, shown below, to measure effectiveness of the program in Fresno.

The J-Scale: Measuring Restorative Justice[5]

Moral wrong of crime is minimized (violation of persons and relationships	Not RJ ‹ 1–2–3–4–5 › RJ	Moral wrong of crime is recognized
Victim, community and offender safety concerns recognized	Not RJ ‹ 1–2–3–4–5 › RJ	Victim/community and offender safety concerns are primary
Disempower victims, offenders and community from acting constructively	Not RJ ‹ 1 – 2 – 3 – 4 – 5 › RJ	Empower victims, offenders and community to act constructively
"Making things as right as possible" is a secondary concern	Not RJ ‹ 1–2–3–4–5 › RJ	Primary focus on "making things as right as possible" (repair injuries, relationships and physical damage)
Primary focus on violation of law	Not RJ ‹ 1–2–3–4–5 › RJ	Violation of law a secondary concern
Victim wounds and healing ignored	Not RJ ‹ 1–2–3–4–5 › RJ	Victim wounds and healing important
Offender wounds and healing ignored	Not RJ ‹ 1–2–3–4–5 › RJ	Offender wounds and healing important

5. 1996. Ron Claassen. "Measuring Restorative Justice," one in a series of papers on restorative justice by Ron Claassen, Co-Director of the Center for Peacemaking and Conflict Studies at Fresno Pacific University and Founding Executive Director of Victim Offender Reconciliation Program of the Central Valley. FPU Center for Peacemaking and Conflict Studies [online]. Fresno, CA: 1996. [Cited August 1, 2002.] Available at ‹http://www.fresno.edu/pacs/docs/jscale.html›.

Primary decisions and activity between offender and government, offender family, victim and community ignored	Not RJ ‹ 1–2–3–4–5 › RJ	Primary decisions and activity between victim and offender (or substitutes) and their communities, with government help as needed
Actions of officials with coercive power or in positions of authority left unchecked	Not RJ ‹ 1–2–3–4–5 › RJ	All actions tested by whether they are reasonable, related and respectful
Government coercive/ authority structures the primary response; victims, community and offender left out of process	Not RJ ‹ 1–2–3–4–5 › RJ	Government coercive/authority structures used as backup when victim or offender not cooperative or either sees the process as unfair
Coercion assumed as primary mode of relating to offenders; orders given to offender rather than inviting offender to be cooperative — no attempt at agreements	Not RJ ‹ 1–2–3–4–5 › RJ	Invitations to offender to be cooperative are primary; agreements preferred over orders; coercion backup response
Placements focus on restrictions and following orders	Not RJ ‹ 1–2–3–4–5 › RJ	Placements focus on safety and/or training and equipping for living in community
Religious/faith community not involved in justice process	Not RJ ‹ 1–2–3–4–5 › RJ	Religious/faith community encouraged and invited into cooperative aspects of justice process

Can the Process Be Too Forgiving?
Parole and Determinate Sentencing

A misconception surrounding restorative justice is that supporters believe in releasing inmates, putting them back out on the streets — as if with a stronger sense of community and spirituality, all crime will end. Not true: restorative justice does not support the release of unfit prisoners.

Rather, it casts light on new judicial processes, and the rights or wrongs therein. The bottom-line theory is that, ultimately, one can begin anew. The question of whether one arrives at restoration "inside" or "outside" depends on the severity of the crime, the prisoner's history and achievements or failures during incarceration. All factors must be evaluated before putting a potential threat into a society filled with potential victims. And so we come to the issue of parole, its past and present, and seemingly ever-changing definition.

There are new laws directing more and more states toward determinate parole.[6] In fact, parole is more likely to be abolished by new statutes of traditional justice than due to the implementation of restorative justice. Eleven states and the federal system have done away with parole, replacing it with what is known as determinate sentencing. Under this latest guideline, a prisoner loses

---

6. A useful discussion of the topic is found in "Determined Demise," Prison Fellowship, 2000, by Elizabeth Carole.

the right to be released, in recognition of his constructive behavior during incarceration, after serving at least a large fraction of his sentence. Instead, a prisoner's release date is set after his sentence begins. The likelihood of the date changing is low, no matter what changes might occur in the inmate's behavior. The national parole failure rate is approximately 60%, so the debate over its viability must be scrutinized further.

Dr. Mario Paparozzi[7] makes claims for both sides. This internationally recognized expert was an assistant professor of law and justice at the College of New Jersey when then-governor Christine Todd Whitman asked him to serve a six-year term as head of the New Jersey State Parole Board with a mandate to straighten out the "mess in the problem-plagued state parole system." Invited in on that basis, he moved swiftly to reduce a backlog of more than 3,000 inmates who had passed their eligibility dates, but hadn't received a hearing. Those who oppose abolishing parole will applaud his efforts.

Most professionals and laymen alike would agree that parole is a privilege rather than a right. Some argue that parole simply means early freedom — unfair freedom. But Paparozzi argues, "We are misunderstanding this whole business about parole and fueling the fires of public anger. [They're] not getting out early if we understand that we've all agreed to the punitive time frame as the first piece of the sentence. What folks need to understand is that the second half of the sentence, where the inmate becomes eligible for parole, is beyond the punitive portion. And if we abolish parole, all we're left with is the punitive portions."[8]

So the question follows — how should our society structure the sentences it imposes? Paparozzi proposes a "two-tiered sentencing structure." This has become a familiar phrase within the United States in

---

7. He served as a parole officer on the streets of Newark in the 1970s; then he spent eight years running the New Jersey State Parole System, leaving as an Assistant Commissioner to serve as National President of the American Probations and Parole Associations. He was also a faculty member at the U.S. National Academy of Corrections before a two year stint as a Union County Freeholder. He retired from parole work in 1998, when he began teaching at the College of New Jersey.

8. Internet Edition, 2002, "Justice and Reconciliation Project," Lisa Rea.

the past years. The first half of the sentence is what the judge expects the criminal to serve in order to pay a debt to society for the crime committed. The latter portion is tacked on for two reasons: to provide a supervised transition period from prison to the streets, and to keep the inmate in prison if his or her conduct has not been such as to earn privileges.

Politicians who want to look "tough on crime" state that abolishing parole has reduced the crime rate in their areas. Paparozzi disagrees, citing how crime continued to soar in the 1970s and 1980s in those states that eliminated parole. Moreover, crime rates *dropped* in states with parole or some other form of conditional release.

The theory comes full circle to suggest that removing the possibility of parole, and using determinate sentencing instead, may head off a violent act as long as the offender remains in custody. Indeed, whatever approach is taken, the chances that a similar crime will be committed with a different victim at a later date will be always problematic unless we examine the root causes of crime.

The "why" behind crime is a key element of restorative justice. This is not about accepting the violence; it is about understanding it, even forgiving it. Determinate sentencing disallows the opportunity for a citizens-oriented parole board to review a criminal's progress prior to his or her release from prison. According to the "two-tiered system," the legitimate need of victims and the general public to know how much time a criminal will serve for a crime is provided; but additionally, everyone will know that there will be a sensible review before the prison gate swings open and the criminal walks out the door into the community, with just the clothes on his back and some change in his pocket. This is definitely not the same as being "soft on crime."

Parole hearings prior to a criminal's release also give victims an opportunity for a full airing of their concerns. The primary mission of parole is to ensure community protection and offender re-integration through vigorous screening and evaluation prior to release. [9]

Finally, how does the parolee prepare for freedom? While some communities are working under the principles of restorative justice, many are still detached from its criminal populous — frightened by stigmas and past tendencies. Paparozzi insists, "preparation [by the prisoner] for parole is key: classes, skills, a plan — where and how to live and work. The more pre-release planning and preparation done, the less the chance the offender will find himself or herself within the category of repeat offenders, behind bars."[10]

---

9. An interesting discussion of the question can be found at http://www.manhattan-institute.org/ html/press_briefing_broken_windows.htm, including a presentation by Paparozzi.

10. Internet Edition, 2002, "Determinate Parole," Michael Paparozzi.

FAITH, RESTORATIVE JUSTICE AND PRISON FELLOWSHIP

Charles W. Colson will argue that, for those who have been sent to prison before, staying out requires maintaining one's faith and following a regimen that adheres, at least in some way, to spirituality. Once a person lands in prison, survival and potential freedom are grounded in the ability to maintain fellowship, in ways that may range from relations with family outside prison, to repentance shown a victim, to actions in everyday prison life.

Colson should know. He is the founder of Prison Fellowship Ministries (an organization that "seeks to solve the intractable issues of crime and violence in America through Christian understanding"). As we celebrate the 25th anniversary of Prison Fellowship, it's almost a miracle itself that Chuck, *aka* the Hatchet Man, an aide to former President Richard Nixon, went from prestige to prison to prayer. In fact, at one time the media described Colson as "incapable of humanitarian thought." Today, he is responsible for reaching out to prison inmates and is working toward reforming the U.S. penal system through his own support of such working concepts as restorative justice. He has authored many books offering his thoughts on how to bring faith into daily life.

Back in 1974, Colson was convicted of white-collar crime; and in his way he was as dangerous as any street criminal, due to his political power. He was found guilty of Watergate-related charges — although not the burglary part of the episode — and voluntarily pleaded guilty to obstruction of justice in the Daniel Ellsberg Case.

Prior to entering Alabama's Maxwell Prison in 1974, he claimed he'd become a Christian. The media jokingly responded that, if "Mr. Colson can repent for his sins, there just must be hope for everybody."[11] Not only was Colson entering the secured facility as a new Christian, but he was the first member of the Nixon Administration to be sent to jail over Watergate. Sentenced to serve up to three years, he was paroled after seven months. However short his term, his experience proved extraordinary, and in a dramatic turnabout, Colson found himself earning the honor that had eluded him in politics: serving the people.

By 1976, Colson was sharing his own spiritual passions through the reach-out program he founded, the Prison Fellowship Ministries. In collaboration with churches of all denominations, this has become the world's largest outreach to prisoners, ex-prisoners, crime victims and their families.

Consistent with the philosophy of restorative justice, Colson came to the conclusion that the connection between offenders and victims should be harmonious, as harmonious as possible while taking full cognizance of what was the foundation of their "relationship." Through fellowship, Colson felt he could not only aid in restoring offenders into communities and help those populaces feel comfortable with such a transition, but equally important, he was bringing an emphasis on religion into the mix. Ultimately, his work marshaled the involvement of the church in prison outreach.

Advocates for restorative justice have called Colson's work "a marked extension in our efforts to ignite a sense of peace and even grace amidst tragedy . . . that the soul is essential in all persons' triumph to find comfort in what is otherwise deemed dark, even irrevocable."[12]

---

11. "Break Point," Radio Commentary, 1974.
12. Why America Doesn't Work, Word Publications, 1991, Jack Eckard.

Colson's work, like restorative justice, is almost seen as policy. His concerns about the efficacy of the American criminal justice system were voiced loudly, making him one of the nations' influential speakers for criminal justice reform. His recommendations have brought legislators from both political parties together to help support efforts to stem the cycle of crimes and poverty so that projects geared toward support might be originated — no matter how large or small. The Angel Tree is one example. This program offers Christmas presents to more than 500,000 children of inmates annually on behalf of their incarcerated parents. With political and private support, Colson has branched out the Angel Tree program, launching a summer camp and other endeavors. The effort of reaching out in a non-critical manner has touched lives globally. Prison Fellowship International was formed in 1979 under Charles Colson's direction. There now exist 88 chapters worldwide. Ironically, after the media passed a dark judgment on his character, he has since been awarded the Humanitarian Achievement honor.[13]

Charles Colson's efforts intertwine with restorative justice, because they also weave their way through this effort. In the following chapters, his influence cannot help but be cited. It is just to recall his participation delving into the greater issues — those reasons why we are forced to set up any criminal system to begin with. To gain insight, issues of family background (mitigating circumstances), worldviews, judicial process (death penalty) and community policy are addressed.

---

13. "Why Believe?," Audio Edition, Lee Strobel, Willow Creek Press.

BRINGING CRIMINALS TO THEIR VICTIMS

A Poor Performance

The *Evansville Courier* (Indiana) has generously given permission to cite a clear example of judicial and interpersonal conflict and confusion that illustrates how those in the criminal justice professions and the community sometimes fail to support the better interests of everyone involved and, by contrast, how they can make a positive difference — often at little cost. This is from *The Evansville Courier*, Monday, February 19, 2001:

> JUDGE JAILS VICTIM IN RAPE CASE AFTER SHE REFUSES TO TESTIFY
>
> A man facing trial for his third felony sex-crime offense got out of jail while his accuser was locked up because she was too frightened to testify against him.
>
> Michelle Robertson spent Tuesday night in jail after Marion Superior Court Judge Patricia Gifford issued an arrest warrant for failing to appear as a witness in court.

Robertson says she'll testify when the rescheduled trial opens on February 26 but was angry about being jailed while the man accused of raping her at knifepoint was released without having to post bail.

"I'm furious that the system is this screwed up," she said.

Ann DeLaney, a former deputy prosecutor who now runs the Julian Center for abused women, said she understood the judge's determination to have the victim at the trial but questioned sending Robertson to jail.

Gifford said Robertson had missed three or four appointments with the defense attorney to give a statement.

"Nobody wants to make a victim (into) a victim twice," she said. "But, unfortunately, within our system of justice, to make it work, you need to come to court to testify. By not appearing, the case becomes impossible."

The accused attacker has two felony sex-crime convictions — for sexual battery in Hendricks County in 1996 and for criminal deviate conduct in Marion County in 1990. In this case, he faces felony charges of rape, burglary, battery and confinement.

Robertson, 34, was attacked last June.

Deputy prosecutor Karen Jensen requested the arrest warrant from Gifford after Robertson failed to show up Monday for the trail. Jensen said she expected Robertson would receive a stern lecture from the judge.

"She said, 'I just can't do this. I can't face him,'" Jensen said of the woman. "She was afraid."

Instead, Robertson was arrested when she came to court the next day, while the defendant was released without bail because of a provision in the state law on speedy trials.

Jensen said she was shocked by the judge's decision to jail Robertson.

"I would have spent the night in jail with her, happily," Jensen said. "It was not right that she had to go."

Robertson said she was now ready to testify. The turning point came Wednesday morning when she got out of jail, was brought into court and had to walk right past her accused attacker.

"I looked over at him," she said. "And then I knew I could do it."

After reading this article, two fundamental questions follow: How else could this have been handled? What happens from here? The harms done, and the needs and obligations that result are central to each of these questions. These issues are pointed out by Jayne Crisp, council to the California's Victim Forum. In her handbook,[14] she emphasizes the importance of acknowledging the victim without ignoring the perpetrator — otherwise, hope of restoration is lost.

The starting point for any restorative justice process is identifying the harms resulting from the crime — in this case, a sexual assault. The Deputy Prosecutor highlighted one harm that the victim was experiencing: fear. The prosecutor suggested that it is this fear that stopped the victim from testifying against the offender.

After having identified the harms, one must ask what the victim needs in order to feel that the harm has been addressed and put right. This victim's needs might have focused on feeling safe again. Her missed appointments with the defense attorney could be seen as sending a message about this fear and the attention that it required. Unfortunately, in this situation, the court disregarded her fear. The court punished her for it, even though it is a harm stemming from the very crime for which

---

14. *Trauma, Surviving Violent Crime: A Handbook For Victims*, 1996, mass market (out of print), Jayne Crisp.

the court wanted to achieve justice. Instead of incarceration or arrest, the victim needed someone to say that they had listened to her expression of fear and that they wanted to know what it would take to help her feel safe again. Her needs may have involved things that the attorneys or other criminal justice personnel could provide. For instance, they could have let her know what to expect in the meeting with the defense attorneys and whether the offender would have been present at this meeting. And their concern and attention to her fear should, of course, not be limited to its impact on her willingness and ability to testify against the assailant.

Not only has the criminal justice system disregarded her fear; it has also denied her a sense of control and empowerment. The sexual assault was already a shocking breach of her sense of control over her life, and now the process that was meant to bring justice to her was beyond her control as well. When she did make a decision on her own — to skip meetings with the defense attorneys — the court made an alternate decision for her and forced her to make an appearance. A restorative process would have recognized her need to start resuming control of her life and would have provided her with opportunities to make informed decisions about the justice process.

A starting place for this "empowerment process" could have involved allowing the victim to make decisions about the conditions under which she would meet with the defense attorneys, about the location and the time of the meeting. Empowerment goes beyond simply making decisions about how and when to do what the criminal justice system demands that one do. It requires a process that respects and facilitates the active participation of the victim, and offender, in a justice process that places at its heart the needs, the harms and the offender's accountability for those harms. The process should give the voice back to the parties involved, offering the opportunity for truth telling, answers, restitution and vindication.

As they say, hindsight is 20/20. We cannot go back and change what has happened in this case. We can ask, however, "What should be done now, after the way this was handled?" It would appear that the victim experienced another wrong, of sorts, through the arrest warrant and incarceration. The process meant to "resolve" a crime may have added insult to injury. It denied her fear and served to dis-empower her. She may be feeling re-victimized and distrustful of the justice system. And, depending on her situation, she may have suffered many other secondary harms as a result.

She may have lost a day's wages or, if she was a single mother, she may have had to pay overnight childcare. In any case, her life was suddenly disrupted and a day was lost; other obligations or plans were interrupted. And a night in jail is traumatic enough, on its own. She may have felt deeply humiliated calling in to work to explain her absence, or facing any neighbors and acquaintances who might have noticed something was wrong.

The restorative justice process would invite offenders to take responsibility for the harms that they caused and the harms she experienced, both by her perpetrator and at the hands of the criminal justice system — both should be addressed by those responsible. How this accountability would be addressed is entirely up to the victim and the justice players. The magic of restorative justice is that it is a worldview that invites each of us to be accountable to others when our actions cause harm, no matter who we are — no matter what the context of our offending.

A Better Way

While Robertson had to come to terms with many issues raised by the way she was treated, she had support of not only the one restorative justice advocate who is mentioned but many others besides.

By way of contrast, here is the story of an even greater tragedy that befell a family, which was however responded to in a more effective manner. (All names have been changed at the requests of individuals involved.)

Sara Carpenter woke at 2:13 AM February 19, 1996, after hearing noise in the house. Startled, she lifted her from her pillow to check the clock, and called out to her daughter, thinking she'd gotten out of bed for a snack.

Tragically, the noise she heard didn't come from her sixteen-year-old, but from two men, both armed, who burst into the bedroom. One put the barrel of his handgun into her husband's mouth while the other shoved his foot into Sara's neck and held his gun to her head. Still another assailant dragged their only child to her parents' room and forced her to strip naked. The men screamed that they would kill the young girl if her mother and father wouldn't "tell where the money was stashed."

The family sobbed, swearing there was no money, no safe. While the disbelieving burglars dragged Sara's husband on a money chase, one stayed behind and sexually violated Sara. "I had my face pressed into the carpet. I prayed aloud and confessed my sins, in case this was it; I needed to confirm my love for God."

Seven years later, Sara reflects that she believed that that was it: she was going to die. "I didn't cry. I didn't scream. A peace came over me . . . I had no fear of death at all. I knew where I was going." She recalls focusing her attention on her daughter; all she could do was to beg them not to harm her further.

"I realized my husband was in sheer terror. He struggled from his knees, trying to protect us." Sara heard a shot, then a thud, and knew what had happened. A fourth young man ran in — the lookout — panicked about a car in the driveway, not realizing it was driven by their own teenaged accomplice. Sara ran to the closet where her husband lay bleeding to death. Her daughter called 911, but there was nothing that could be done.

Today, unlike that summer night in 1992, she does weep as she relives the crime. She's remarried, with a new life, but willing to relive her nightmare as often as it takes, as long as there are other victims who can benefit from her story, and take inspiration from her spirit to survive and move forward.

"I tell my story because I want restorative justice. Criminals are held accountable for the damage they inflicted on their victims, allowing the victims the healing salve of participating in the process, and providing offenders real incentive to change."

For 22 months after the break-in, the rape and the murder, Sara sat in her courthouse hallway — called in to testify during the trials but banned from the courtroom the remainder of the time. She recalls that "To be left out wasn't fair, it wasn't . . . healing." So Sara began to take advantage of every court recess to go into the trial area and peek. "The district attorney was kind about keeping me informed, as well." It gave her a "sense of power," something that was sadly lacking in the previous case.

"There is nothing remarkable [in her gaining that sense of empowerment], in fact, [it is] absolutely anticipated if specific guidelines — as were — followed,"[15] remarks Dr. Paul McCold, Director of Research for the International Institute for Restorative Practices, Bethlehem, Pennsylvania.

Sara was allowed to make a victim-impact statement during sentencing for her daughter's rapist. Under pressure from restorative justice supporters, California state legislation had passed a victims' rights bill providing this opportunity. Considering the support that had made it possible for her to have this opportunity, Sara reflects that she "had to keep in motion with the ideology that allowed her a voice."

Sara sat close to the defendant, out of the camera's eye. "I was able to address the defendant. I had memorized what I wanted to say . . . It

---

15. Peacemaking/Human Relations In Corrections, 4th Ed., Waveland, 1998, Dr. Paul McCold.

was so hard at first, but then, as the words came out, I realized my feelings and it was incredibly actuating." Sara explicitly described the event, and how it had harmed her and her family, and stolen her husband from them. "I bared my soul, going all the way back to my own childhood, and how I'd suffered abuse then and how this related to similar emotional issues for me. I also knew that by bringing up my own sordid past, they [the defense] lost that card, had they intended to play it: pity." Sara told the rapist that she didn't deny that something horrific must have happened to him to make him do what he'd done, but he had to recognize choice, and live with consequence.

Not only had Sara been victimized, but also the courts, until finally allowing her to have the last word, had left her out of the loop. As well, "People who knew me sidestepped me, some chastised me for not grieving 'properly' — and for not replacing the blood-stained carpet right away. But I wanted people to understand: this man poured out his blood for me — why should I be shook up because his blood was on my carpet?"

Left to survive with $10,000 in life insurance and few job skills, Sara was scared. But then, new forces, restorative forces entered her life. Mark Junt, president of her husband's place of employment, offered to pay for legal fees and provide food for three years. "Produce companies don't have community affairs departments!" she chuckles. But Mark's action stemmed from more than a desire to help a friend. He felt "that (my) company was a responsible part of the community, and needed to take an assertive role to help stop the violence, to help the victim without getting involved with chastising the criminal. That had to be compartmentalized."

Sara takes her friend's lead, making a point to speak to juveniles and other offenders and victims alike. Her heart has not grown cold to the outcast, the "lost soul." She insists that criminal-justice approaches that help restore and heal victims also help restore offenders and the community. "Without people to help offenders realize their damage, there will never, never be change."

In the late 1990s, Sara had the opportunity to meet the girl who drove the get-away car. At the California Youth Authority, with the help of a trained mediator, Sara went through the crime once again. Realizing the driver hadn't seen the nightmare from her position, she says, "She needed to know what she'd been a part of."

The young inmate listened, cried, and apologized. "There was peace. We moved forward. She was a child. She wants degrees, now, she wants her life, and she had no idea the damage [she caused]. I can't lie and say I don't resent on some level, imagining again my daughter forced to strip . . . but I work on my forgiveness. I thank God for the opportunity to work through this, rather than the void of never knowing, never speaking out, never having any rights . . . and that comes to me through restorative justice." She went on to explain that the process helps personalize the actions, countering the natural tendency toward detachment (which may offer some protection, but is not necessarily healing). "She's a real being. It's harder to hate. It's part of the human condition: hard to hate someone we've reached some level of intimacy with, even if for only three hours."

Next, Sara plans a meeting with the man who pinned her to the floor. He apologized in court, and Sara told him in no uncertain terms to "prove it." He is up for parole in 2009, but Sara isn't frightened. "I hope I'm a part of his process. I hope by then he's graduated from high school and has some direction; I hope I can help."

While the murderer received life imprisonment, Sara wishes him a productive life. She's forgiven him also, while still feeling that this is his destiny. He took life; he'll have to make his work from prison. Speaking for herself, she says, "I don't know, I suppose it's a matter of readjusting: making new friends (and a new husband), and embracing those supporters within my community, embracing my spirituality. As we carry our cross, He carries us . . . Restoring life."

An issue that restorative justice faces is the opinion that to forgive, to even hope that a criminal can be put back into a community, to live and function and learn to associate with mainstream, is horrific. After all, once a man or woman crosses the legal line, especially in felonious cases, doesn't the person lose all rights to live amongst the general populace?

According to supporters of restorative justice, to define any human being as some sort of creature who belongs in a cage is to take away his or her humanity — not to mention what he may be able to give back to his victim, should he be allowed a chance to operate and become, even if for the first time, productive.

Such issues come down to simple basic questions: Do prisons deter criminals? Are offenders punished because they deserve to be punished, or are they punished beyond an appropriate time span, to make a social point?

Reformist Chuck Colson has his own story, suggesting possible answers.

"My first day in prison remains vivid in my memory, particularly the moment I was ushered into the office of my case-worker, the official who had my life in his hands. If this bureaucrat was intimidated to be facing the former special counsel to the President of the United States, he didn't show it. 'All right, Colson,' he said, leaning back in his government-issued swivel chair. 'Let me tell you what this prison is about.' The he sharply slapped the back of his left hand with his right hand. 'That's it,' he said with a toothy grin.

"I didn't need to be treated like a child, I wanted to tell him (but didn't). Yet over the years, I've come to realize that in his simple way he expressed a profound — but often ignored — truth: and it is one that is central to the renewed debate over punishment, including capital punishment." [16]

The question that drove Colson was, What is right punishment? This question is highly charged, for most of us. It creates arguments over dinner and political debates between family members, and while we may sit in our secure environments discussing punishment, and life and death, some people are dying and other people are missing their parole dates because the paper work passed by, tossed into the garbage while the inmate's family sat waiting with bated breath for the hope of any good news. Prison punishment is never a casual topic. It's painful and dangerous.

In the literature debating issues of punishment, books and scholarly articles alike, behind every theory justifying prisons and punishment and every theory cautioning to avoid excessive punishment lies the conundrum — what is just and what is not? The liberal arena fights for restoration and rehabilitation while law-and-order conservatives staunchly declare that deterrence is the only method that works. Ironically, as Colson explains, both have "contributed to the prison-building boom, the population doubling in the last ten years." Thus, "If nothing else has been learned, we can now assess that external argument is not mending the criminal issues that plague our communities. And yet, simultaneously these arguments are utilitarian — people looking toward the same goal: a more fit society." [17]

---

16. "Punishment." 12 Internet Edition, "Surviving or Not — the Eternal Conflict, Literally," Nov. 1999, Sara James.
17. "What is Just," Internet Edition, Chuck Colson Speaks, 2001.

"My caseworker was making a different point (than jointly looking toward ways to cap criminal behaviors): that is, an offender is punished because he deserves it."

This is what C. S. Lewis, in his essay, "The Humanitarian Theory of Punishment," called "just deserts." Referring to the deterrent theory, Lewis asked, "Why in heaven's name am I to be sacrificed to the good of society in this way? Unless, of course, I deserved it?" He concludes, "Take away desert and the whole morality of punishment disappears." To justify punishment by whether it deters or cures is the triumph of sociology over justice.

Lewis, and Colson's caseworker, cut to the heart of the matter — and their point directs our attention toward the issue of capital punishment. "For most of my life, both as a Christian and before, I opposed the death penalty. I worried about innocent defendants being found guilty. As a lawyer, I knew that happened. But most importantly, I could find no [evidence that it served as a] deterrent."

Jeff Sachs, a California defense attorney, was recently asked, "Why handle the defense of murderers?" He reflects on his first case, when he was in his mid-thirties, almost thirty years ago. His client, Lonnie, had been accused of throwing a girl into the bed of his pick up truck and taking her to a remote area in northern California, where he raped her repeatedly. He was arrested and tried. On the stand, the rather large young woman pointed to the defendant, adamant that he was her assailant. Trouble is, Lonnie is not a large man. The defendant was asked,

> "How tall are you, and what is your weight?"
>
> "5'4" and 190 pounds. Why?"
>
> Jeff held out a photograph. "Does this look like Lonnie?"
>
> "It's a headshot, but yes — just more clear [than another photo]."
>
> "Madam, this man is 6'4", weighing 220 pounds. *He* is your rapist."

The young attorney actually wept when he saw his client spared a near life sentence and returned to freedom. His response to skeptics ever since has been, "If there's a single innocent defendant, I need to make sure he won't be put to death. And if I'm wrong, I'm not so stupid that my conscience hasn't known that weight — when I've picked up the paper only to read one of my freed clients is back in county jail on rape charges. Still, my passion is to keep people alive. Innocent people. The world is weighed so that all people are protected. I suppose I was meant to be on this side, no matter the scrutiny."

Colson is fast to acknowledge the downside to his anti-death position, no matter how strong his politics and spirit are. "I went to death row in Illinois in the mid-1980s [to counsel inmates] and began having doubts about my position. John Wayne Gacy, convicted of the brutal murders of 33 men and boys, asked to see me. He spent most of our one-hour conversation insisting on his innocence, angry at the state for how he was treated. I was struck by his unrepentant arrogance. (It struck me that) his was a pitifully inadequate sentence for such horrid crimes. Hardly heavy enough to balance Lady Justice's scales. Lewis's questions hounded me: What is the 'just desert' for such heinous crimes?"

But in time, despite such confusion, Colson, as well as this author and many others who have worked with societal "monsters" concede that, after the shock dissipates, the theory of grace remains. Colson is a thinking man, who weighs the subtleties of the issue carefully; because he adheres to a biblical philosophy that allows that in specific, very rare cases, capital punishment must be considered, he leaves the door open to that possibility. Others among us remain steadfast in believing that death is death. There is no gray area.

Bob Smith, whose daughter was killed after being abducted and raped by Gene Bell in 1985, watched as the news announced his execution in 1996. "There was no sense of closure. I prayed for his parents. Nothing could bring [Shari] back."

Certainly no other criminal justice issue, and few issues in general, generate more controversy than the death penalty. It's easy to understand — at least "lifers" don't force us to take permanent responsibility, or to make choices perhaps only meant for God.

"The execution of a human being is an extraordinarily powerful, emotional event," an anonymous ACLU member has remarked. "It reminds us that we are all doomed to die. It reminds us vicariously of what it must be like: choosing another's time to die. Statistically, there exists little evidence to back up the ideology that death provides vindication.

"With my son's perpetrator lost, I had no one to hate . . . and I still needed someone to hate. Now, I want answers. Perhaps I could have asked him why? Moreover, if nothing could be resolved by his living, what possibly was resolved by his death?"

So while Chuck Colson will, for the sake of religion (which is core to restorative justice) allow that at the root of justice is not sociology or therapy but "just desserts," the next chapter reveals (while not a murder case) why sociology is actually the root of most evil.

LINDA'S STORY, A MEMOIR

What is the experience, what are the driving forces, what are the feelings of a perpetrator? Linda Taylor has shared an excerpt from her upcoming book, A Rat's Tale, so that we might examine a true life account of a female prison inmate, from childhood to release from jail. Throughout the retelling of her capture, prosecution, incarceration and preparation for release, the "angels" and "demons" of control and absence of control over her own fate and her own actions, over what she was doing and what was being done to her or even "for" her, illustrate how the principles of Restorative Justice bring mental health and responsibility to the process, and how damaging can be the traditional punitive methodologies that emphasize control by external forces.

After a criminal is caught, we consider that there might be shame and guilt, but it may be thrill that drives the offender — while shame may come later. Linda's life had those moments — those events we all know, when we feel our paths shifting, just so slightly. She reveals such details, and through her depiction it becomes evident how one misguided step might lead to the next, until, finally, it feels like there is nowhere left to step toward. Pressed into a corner, with no choice, no more room for maneuver in any direction.

Linda Taylor allowed poor self-esteem to become the manifestation of her entire person. A lack of self and lack of family provided an open door to a life that dropped to the depths, one step at a time. From anger to drugs to theft to felony to promiscuity and finally apprehension, Linda has seen the world through the eyes of the convict. She is the woman we might have feared. She is also the woman today we would more likely embrace.

How do such things start? I was the elder of two little girls, born and raised in southern California and for the most part, very cheerful, bright and normal. My family was dysfunctional in that all-American way so many of us pretend to understand. I was tormented with thoughts about many things that seemed important to my parents — yet not to me. I felt the need to impress, to test the waters, even as a child. I hated the pressure to be "normal." Not to mention, it all seemed like a game, from social issues to religion — my parents were lax Catholics; but still wanted to go to church on the "big days" and send me to Catechism classes.

I think that was the first time I was defiant — and independent of my parents: I was about 5 years old. I despised those classes and my soul had plainly been telling me that I could not be spoon-fed this theology that did not resonate with me. I was only about 5 at the time, so none of this was well-formulated. I had no REAL arguments for my bewildered parents, so I was willing to get into a lot of trouble to staunchly REFUSE to attend these classes. We moved from California to Rhode Island when I was around seven years old. My parents had too much to do to worry about Catechism classes anymore.

But this religion thing wasn't my biggest oddity. My dad had really wanted a boy and, well, I am a girl. He loved me and we were close, but we did "boy" things together. I tried to be a good "son" for him, but I could only keep that up for so long; any thoughts of being "good" were not happening after I turned about 11 or so. I was a smart little girl. I loved to read and I had tons of stuffed animals. I disliked dolls. Come on, I was a boy, right? I loved horses and actually was fortunate enough to have one — thanks to my dad — who always spoiled me with gifts. Emotionally, he was not available, so

44

he bought my sister and me stuff instead. From him and from the World. I had not been shown much different, yet.

We moved from Rhode Island to Pennsylvania and then back to California again in the space of 2-1/2 years. I was in fifth grade and in the advanced sixth grade math and English classes. Not a raving genius, but sharp with burgeoning possibilities. My dad had been grooming me to be the class president, as well the President of the United States. There was a new program for smart kids called Mentally Gifted Minors. Of course, they had me take this IQ test, demanding a certain level for the program. I figured I am a shoe-in. I took the test and scored an IQ level of 132. High, not high enough: my dad was . . . incensed — or embarrassed, I'm not sure. I needed at least a 134, so at only 132, I was out. I was okay with it, but my dad was in denial that I was not a "genius." He called the school and bitched and made them give me second test. I was so embarrassed. I felt I wasn't good enough. Smart enough. A failure at 11 years old. What was the use of continuing to do any good? It sounds so cliché now — not at eleven.

I started to withdraw. My parents were fighting all the time by now, so that also made me more prone to keep to myself and my friends, not family. It was an unhappy time, but nothing changed on the surface. The illusion of normalcy was intact. I cared less about school. I started thinking about guys and ways to get into trouble; just small things, but I was becoming increasingly rebellious and angry inside. When I was 13, my parents divorced. I was already pissed off, at my dad especially, and I ran away — acting out my anger and confusion. I hitchhiked around southern California for a day and a half, then, both tired and broke, went home. My dad flipped out and wanted to call the cops and have me thrown in juvenile hall or something equally frightening. Tough Love.

Well my mom would hear none of that, and while she was distraught, she also always loved me unconditionally, and was not about to abandon me. I was living with my mom; my sister went with my dad, for whatever reason. She told me recently it was because I was so mean to her. I don't remember.

But by this time, I was medicating myself, using marijuana and other harder drugs. I fell for a guy, and lost my virginity at 14, after smoking almost an ounce of crappy weed before I had the nerve to do the deed. It was a horrible experience ... I continued in this vein, sneaking out of my house and walking for miles to see this guy, who surely did not deserve any of my attentions. I was listening to lots of hard rock and snorting kanebenol, an elephant tranquilizer. I had been playing guitar for a year by then and once I heard punk rock, in 1978, that was it. I had found my niche. I was already hanging out with older people than me, mainly guys. I did not relate well to other girls. I was having sex with whomever I liked, doing drugs and all of my friends were in bands. I was a bad-ass punk-rocker chick — young and cute, messed up and looking for fun. I was already an outlaw. This was the start of feeling untouchable, above rules, the law. My mom was at my mercy; she had to go back to work and I was a wild thing. I got kicked out of high school during my freshman year, because I never went to class; they stuck me in this afternoon program, remedial work. I was in heaven.

Then, for a "challenge" — when I made too many credits, they stashed me in a different program, something for smart but troubled teens. I cared more about getting stoned, and music. When I was 16, and at the end of my sophomore year, I talked my mom into the California High School Equivalency Exam. She consented, when I agreed to at least take a couple of classes at the junior college. I passed the test. I enrolled at Fullerton JC to take classes in philosophy, art and music.

I met Rikk there, who would be my dear friend and lover for years. Rikk was in numerous bands and through him and what I was doing musically, I met everyone. Him and a guy named Robert were the very first punk rockers in Orange County. I also got tight with Robert and joined his band, the Omlits. I was coming into my own and music, drugs, my friends and their acceptance of me were all I cared about. Being a punk rocker is a lifestyle choice and I reveled in the attention it gave me. I was the baddest chick in our circle of friends and I gloried in this fact, doing any stunts that would garner me more of the spotlight. I would show up home at 5 AM and fall into bed. My mom did not know what to do with me. I was smoking pot in the house, in front of her. I was getting away with it. I did not care about anything except what I wanted. Being with my friends, gaining their approval and respect was my whole focus and I went to great lengths to continue to garner more attention.

The first time I got arrested was proof I was spinning out of control. The night it happened, I singing for this all-girl punk band called IUD at a club. I was 17 or 18 — and had been drinking beer all night. A sloshed marine starts haranguing us for being punk rockers, saying all sorts of rude crap to us. "Who is this asshole?" Carl, a biker-friend, asked. He was nobody to mess with. This marine zero's in on Robert, who was gay and semi-strange looking. He starts taunting him with slurs and then lunges and whacks him in the head and Robert's glasses go flying off and he kind of steps back, dazed. Carl whips out his knife and goes ice cold.

I just tried to stop it: "Hey, Carl, drop it. This jerk's not worth it."

The dude ran off. So we get more beer and go back outside to bitch about it. We were in the back of the lot when the cops show up. My dad was always calling cops, "them pigs," so I followed suit. They jumped out of the cars, two of them.

"Whose beer is this?"

I kicked the beer over. "What beer?"

One of the cops tried to grab me and I started screaming to "leave me alone!" Just ranting, furious, and they're trying to grab me and I'm kicking and throwing punches and cursing and Carl and Robert are yelling at the cops to let me go. It was like this wild animal inside myself came out and all the rage and confusion I was feeling about life just culminated in that instant and I was an uncontrollable, furious beast. They wrestled handcuffs on me and dragged me to the cop car and threw me in the back. I started kicking and throwing myself against the door and windows. No real escape there. Driving to the jail, I quieted down — I did not have an audience and was sitting passively in the back, waiting. I had no idea what I was being charged with and I did not have the presence of mind to ask. I did not really care. Somewhere between screams, they had read me my rights. I got finger-printed, turned over everything in my possession and got escorted to a cell with several women and the door slammed shut. It felt horrible; dirty and desperate, and bleak and lifeless, barren, cold and there was no way to get comfortable. I must tell you what I looked like that night. I was wearing my hair in wild, spiked shag and it was a magenta purple color. I had on flimsy lingerie with a long, black leather coat and thigh-high boots. I had on punkish/Egyptian makeup; I always applied eyeliner to my eyes like an Ancient Egyptian. I looked wild and slutty and punk rock to the hilt. Total nightmare feeling in there. Real dark energies, hopelessness, despair, resignation.

I call my mom. What a lousy call to have to make at 4:00 in the morning. She is relieved to hear from me, and then bummed to hear where I am. She will come and bail me out. I feel a stab of empathy about what I am putting my mom through. Then, instantly, I am thinking about myself and when can she get me out of here? I am led back to a cell, but they go into a different area now and stick me in with these three or four tough-looking Hispanic chicks. They are glaring. They growl some rude remarks at me and back off. I curl up again in a sort of neutral corner of the small cell and try to go back to sleep until my mom can get me out. I felt pure misery. So this is the reality of defiance and rebellion. No more bravado about defying cops and jail.

I dozed off and on, watching my back, and finally five hours later a guard came to the door and unlocked it, yelling my name. Later that afternoon, me and my mom drove over to Robert's to get my car. He just grinned wickedly at me and gave me the keys. He said he thought I had been magnificent the night before and he was in awe. I had nothing good to say about that first jail experience to him but I lied and said it was all no big deal, no one could break me, ever. But it had really brought me down; it felt low. But since I wasn't good enough for anything great anymore, what the hell?

The repercussions of that night were nada, so I learned nothing from the experience. Ironically, it did really heighten my reputation as a punk chick; everyone heard the story from Robert. I was so cool. This was where I became an icon of sorts and people around me began emulating my behaviors, which only served to make me want to take it all even further, for the attention, approval, the newfound respect I had in the eyes of my peers. I did things that even made them wary of how unpredictable I was becoming and to what lengths I would go to shock and outrage, even my so-called friends. Robert and I had a blow up at some point and I recruited a new singer for the band and then he decides to get into heroin. I had been through too many people, seen too much of the underbelly, done so much drugs and I was just tired of everything. Already completely jaded at 19 or 20 years old. That was basically the last straw for me and playing music, at least for awhile. I was changing too, but I attributed that to the world around me, not to any internal struggles I may have had going on. I tried hard not to think about the important issues in my life. I had to get a real job. So for the time being I was out of the bands, and just trying to find out what was next for me, if the music thing had played out.

I had befriended a guy named Danny in my one semester of Junior College and stayed friendly with him throughout these passing years. It was a working relationship — he dealt the best pot in southern California and always had it. I worked several jobs and then got into a line I did well at: purchasing agent in the aerospace industry. I dealt with inventory and contracts and bids; and I actually liked it. My forte was working in distribution. I was stoned morning, noon, and night. I functioned wonderfully. No one suspected. The job was bringing me more money than I ever had playing music and allowed me to party as much as I wanted. I was living with my mom in an apartment; we shared rent and utilities. She had gotten used to the pot. My friend Rikk would spend weekends with me and we would hole up in my room and smoke pot and snort cocaine, which I got from my pal Danny.

I was laid off of my aerospace job. I was compensated pretty well, and I had a 401K that I cashed in. Danny had been talking to me about dealing some pot for him. He did not want to sell small quantities anymore; he was ready to branch out and he thought that it would be a great thing for both of us. I saw what was out there, as far as work, which was not much. I told him that I wanted to do it. Once I was ensconced as a dealer for Danny, he started sending people to me who wanted anything under an ounce. In no time, I paid him back for the half pound and I was making money and socking it away, as well as having the best buds, free. I did not think at all about how much trouble I could get in, or what the hell I was doing with my life. No one came over that I did not already know, and I was careful. I was out of work, but making more money than I ever had before. Life's little ironies. Crime can pay. This is what I was seeing firsthand and the experience was changing me and honing the antisocial, outlaw attitudes I was already fostering into something solid and concrete that would leave an indelible imprint.

I met Joe in 1987. I was 25 years old. I was just hit by the fabled thunderbolt. I had to talk to him, touch him. It was love at first sight. He played in a band and asked me to join. Then he moved on in. Joe and I shared a room and his previous roommates, Mick and Boz, took the second bedroom. We jammed in a basement studio and we would snort speed and play all night long. I was back in my element with these three fantastic guys, making music and connecting, yet on a higher level than I had previously done. I was working at a decent job again. Then, one Tuesday evening, Joe and I wound up being arrested in our apartment.

I was sitting at our dining room table drawing and watching TV. I had just rolled a tasty joint and Joe and I were waiting for Mick and Boz to come home. It sounded like someone was shouting across the hall at this neighbor's apartment. Mick and Boz came in. Then it got quiet and I was about to spark up my joint when there was a knock at our door. Mick cracked the door. It was the cops. I stashed the joint quickly. The cops forced open the door and spotted a bong on the table. They pushed their way into the apartment now, saying they had probable cause to come in because of the drug paraphernalia. So these cops were in our living room, and they start asking us questions about this neighbor across the hall. How well did we know him, had we seen him that evening, blah, blah, blah.

The cops were scoping out the apartment. Telling us to stay where we were, they began to search the place. We had dope growing in our apartment, and I had at least an ounce of marijuana in my room. One of them turned to me. Did I share my room with anyone? We headed that way; I turned around and this cop had found a chunk of hash. I had actually forgotten it was there. They still hadn't noticed the bright light coming from the hall closet. Finally, the one who had been searching my room came out. He was empty-handed, except for the hash. He had not found my ounce. The other cop was looking in this other closet-type thing and he came out with this dusty pair of nun-chucks. He asked us whose they were. Joe said they were his. Well, it turns out these martial arts implements were illegal, considered a lethal weapon. Joe and I were under arrest.

I was not going to resist or do anything stupid. One cop handcuffed my hands behind my back while the other did the same to Joe. Then, one cop finally notices the brilliant light; he opens the door, and sees this growing apparatus with this one little tiny pot plant struggling to live in it. Joe was telling Boz and Mick to get a hold of his dad. He was a bail bondsman. Joe also mentioned our ATM cards were in my purse and they could withdraw the money to bail us out of jail. I was numb, myself. It really sucked to be handcuffed in your home then led by cops in the apartment building you lived in. Definitely a humiliating experience, and it had just been bad luck. They drove us to jail and we were separated for the booking procedure. I got fingerprinted and thrown into a cell. I had faith in Mick and Boz that they would do everything possible to make sure we got out tonight. And after about five hours, we were freed.

In mid-November of the same year, Joe was very badly hurt on his motorcycle. He was in the hospital for three weeks, during Thanksgiving and into December. The band virtually ground to a halt. It was a terrible ordeal. He was dealing with this attorney and he was going to settle for $100,000. The lawyer would get a third. I was spending all my time at the hospital with Joe. It was decided that Joe and I would move together to San Clemente and that Mick and Boz would do their own thing. The band was history. Joe and I started spending more time with Danny. Around this time, Joe received the money for his injury. Danny had been talking to Joe about investing part of his money in a hydroponic marijuana grow unit he was also investing in. Joe's decision altered the course of our lives, but we were already heading in that direction; it did speed things up. Within the next few days I went to see a clued-in lawyer about the search and seizure laws. He listened to what had happened and told me that I had a strong case. He wanted a $1500 retainer, so I gave him a credit card. Joe had no money to pay an attorney, so he was going to have to take whatever the judge threw at him. I could only help myself. The day of the hearing came. First, Joe was going to have to plead no contest to the possession of the illegal weapon that they had charged him with. The judge gave him three years of informal probation. My turn was next. My lawyer asked me all the right questions, and even though I came off like a furious, defiant brat, the judge dismissed the charges against me. He said the police had acted without probable cause and the search of our apartment was inadmissible. We partied that night like fiends. We also went down to our practice place and played our asses off, snorting speed and smoking lots of pot, celebrating our victory against the "Man." Life went on; playing music in the studio — we made a tape and were prepared to begin playing in the LA clubs.

Joe invested his money, about $50,000, and he started spending time with Danny in the unit. Danny was doing some other illegal stuff besides the grow unit (and these units were warehouse sized operations — not small stuff) and was traveling once in awhile to El Paso and doing jobs for a guy called Sid. I met Sid's "woman," Kimmy, and I started doing little favors for her, like renting cars in my name for her to use. Kimmy and Danny came to Joe and I with a new idea; the plan was to rent a nice house in Laguna Miguel under a fake name and Joe and I would move in. We would convert the garage into an extension of the warehouse grow unit. We would have five or six "mommy" plants to take cuttings from. Danny was doing more stuff for Sid in El Paso and was gone frequently. He had a new girlfriend and one day she calls me at the house, hysterical, saying that Danny has been arrested in Texas. I thought fast. His truck was in my name. The pagers he had on him, I had got for him too. I calmly called the pager places and cancelled the service. I sat down with Joe and we discussed the glaringly obvious: that we were in over our heads. We decided that for now, we would stay at the house and, depending on Danny, we would continue to re-evaluate our situation. We were so very naïve.

He actually managed to get bailed out of jail and he came home. He seemed edgy — he was acting erratically. Kimmy was also starting to act strange. She gave me the money every month to pay the rent and the bills for the house — one month I could not get a hold of her, and I was getting really concerned about some of the bills that were not going to be paid. When she finally did call, she was cold, and I hung up feeling like we needed to get the hell out of Dodge City.

Things got worse. Danny called me and told me to get over to his house: he has these two boxes of pot he needs me to stash at my house for him, that it's no good for him to have it at home when he is still in all this trouble. Then I get a phone call from a very irate Kimmy. She starts ranting to me that Goddamn Danny has ripped her off for a lot of pot and do I know anything about it? I had to stay calm. I called Danny — I said I did not want to know, just get this weed out of my house. Then I get a phone call from the infamous Sid. He starts threatening he will kill Joe and I if this situation is not resolved. I shot back I had no knowledge of what the hell he was talking about. I wanted to get out of the house and far away from Sid; I had no idea what the man was capable of doing to us.

Joe came home and I filled him in. We heard a car pull into the driveway and I thought it was Danny, coming to get the stolen cannabis. But no, it was Kimmy, in a foul mood over this whole weed thing. We took her out into the garage and she saw that everything there was fine, thriving in fact, and she really got nice. She excitedly shows us her brand new Explorer and starts blasting the stereo in it and drives away. She even gave me the money for the house expenses. I was not fooled, however, by her pleasant demeanor. Things here were getting hot. And we didn't know why, or what was really going on. That's the drug world for you.

During this time, Joe had begun talking to a man in New Jersey called Rudy. He was the main investor in the warehouse unit, and he started working with Joe, assisting him in the running of the grow unit via telephone. Rudy was now also distrustful of Danny and wanted Joe and I to slowly break away from him. At this point, I started talking to Rudy myself. It was the beginning of an intense and secret relationship between he and I. It would last about 5 months, but it ended with a bang.

More to the point, this was the starting point of our professional relationship. It would be more exciting and challenging than anything I had ever done. Rudy had just gotten busted himself, and was looking at 25 years in prison. Rudy had never mentioned this to Joe in their dealings, but once we started getting to know him, he let us in on everything, literally. One of the things he did after we talked for the first time was to FedEx us SkyPagers. Then money; to the tune of $5,000. I was instructed to purchase certain items; long, black wig; round-trip airline tickets to Newark, New Jersey; and contracts for three voice mail services that I would use later on. When Rudy and I spoke again several days later, he wanted to know if I had accomplished everything. I had, and was ready. I gave him my itinerary but I still had no idea what I was actually going to do for him. I flew out one night during the second or third week of September, in 1993. I was thirty years old. It was the beginning of the end.

I rented a car and drove into New Jersey. I headed for the diner where I was to meet Rudy. I sat down and ordered some coffee. I was to be pleasantly surprised: Joe had only described Rudy to me as he looked in disguise on the day he had met with him at the warehouse. A man walks up to my table, looks at me and then slides into the seat across from me. It was Rudy. He was wearing his infamous fat suit. He had a baseball hat on and he wore glasses. He had a nice looking face and a pleasant smile. He began telling me that he had a few things for me and that we would go over some now and some later when I had checked into a hotel. He handed me a map of the area. He had already picked a house in the area he wanted me to rent — that was my "job," for now. After this initial meeting, it was my problem to run all the small details down. Rudy gave me the advertisement from the newspaper of the townhouse he wanted me to get. I got a room, showered, and made myself at home. Then I called the people renting the house and made arrangements to see the place that same afternoon. Rudy gave me a paper with a woman's name on it and a social security number. Rudy said this would be the name that I was to use to rent the house. He explained that the SS number was this woman's, and that her credit would be good. The last thing he handed over was my first fake driver's license. I got out the nice outfit that I had brought to rent the house. The idea was that I was pretending to be Kimmy. Rudy knocked on the door about an hour after that. He was delighted that I had things under control. We sat down and talked about the story of the person that I was pretending to be: where I was from, what I did for a living and why I needed a place in New Jersey. I voiced my concern that this guy would want to see some identification before he would rent his house to me, but Rudy just smiled and assured me business cards alone would do the trick. He left to make the business cards. I changed into the outfit and fixed my makeup, to attempt to look as much like Kimmy as I could. I heard a knock on the door of the hotel room. Rudy was back. I was dying to see his reaction to how I looked in my disguise. Rudy was absolutely speechless.

I met the guy I had spoken to and he gave me a tour. I explained the company I worked for was moving operations from southern California to the New Jersey area. I told him I liked the place and was interested in renting it. I handed him one of the business cards Rudy had printed for me. He said he would check my references Monday. I had pulled it off. I paged Rudy right away. Three grand for this? Rudy was flirting, telling me I should buy something sexy to wear: he would love to see me in or out of it. First thing Monday morning, I called the voice mails. Each one had a message from the owner of the house, checking my job and home references. I paged Rudy and told him I needed help. Rudy said that he would act as my employer. His girlfriend would call on another one, pretending to be my landlord. I took a shower, got dressed, and then I called the voice mails again to check to see if there were any new messages. Both messages had the owner of the house calling back to let me know that my credit was good and he was awaiting my call. I called the man and asked if I could sign the lease and get the keys to the house as soon as possible. I paged Rudy and when he called back, I was happy to inform him about my good news. Rudy was impressed at how well I had done. He wanted to take me out to celebrate my success. When Rudy came to pick me up that night for dinner, it was sans the fat suit. At dinner, Rudy told me he was married and had three children. Rudy claimed that his wife was sexless, and that he had been cheating on her on and off for about three or four years; he also had a girlfriend that he loved. Rudy started telling me about how he had been fantasizing about me since that first morning we had met. Rudy grabbed me and kissed me. That was the beginning. When my flight finally landed in Orange County, Joe was there to meet me. When we got home, I gave him the keys to the house and the map that Rudy had given to me to help him to find the place when he got out there. I explained what it was like in New Jersey. Rudy had told Joe to go down to Laguna to round up the Mexicans he needed for Rudy's scheme. Before he could do this, though, I needed to don my Kimmy disguise and go to the airport and rent a car for Joe to use when he was with the Mexican guys. After, I would drive by and give it to Joe to use. Then I had to go to several different travel agents in various towns and secure plane tickets for Joe and all the Mexican guys he was going to take with him to Jersey. Rudy had sent Joe another FedEx package filled with money while I was away. Joe and I knew these Mexicans would not be flying back, but it was important that they thought that they would. Joe would "hire" the Mexicans and keep them busy somehow for a couple of hours, while I was running around purchasing tickets. As soon as I had bought them, I was to page Joe and we would meet in a place so I could give him the tickets. Rudy had advised Joe to purchase a pair of black, nerdy looking glasses with a tint to hide his true eye color and a nondescript base-ball hat to wear. That way, the Mexicans could not be able to positively identify Joe when they got arrested in the house in New Jersey. Rudy had said that, since these Mexican guys were illegal aliens, that they would not actually be charged with any crime when they were arrested, just deported back to their country. The day after Joe had left for New Jersey, I paged Rudy on a pay phone. I was very anxious to find out how Joe was doing and if everything was over. Rudy called me back right away. He was excited. Everything had gone just great and it would make all the newspapers in the New Jersey area. It had been a big bust and a total success. I asked him when I would be coming out there again. Rudy said that he would need me out there soon, but that he wanted Joe and I to get moved into a new place first. I found the perfect place from an ad in the paper and I got right to work.

Because of the problems with Danny, Sid and Kimmy, Joe had taken one or two of the best cuttings from each of the varieties of marijuana that we were growing in the garage unit. One day my pager went off and it was Rudy. He told me that he wanted me to rent a house in Tucson, Arizona for some guy he knew. Rudy said it was for someone I would be working with in the near future. When I finally reached the owner of the house, I introduced myself and told him that both my sister and I were interested in relocating to the Tucson area. My sister had been checking out the Tucson classifieds for a suitable house and had seen his ad and driven down to check out the house. She had told me that it was exactly what we were looking for. He described the interior and exterior of the house to me in great detail in our conversa-tion. He inquired as to what I did for a living and how soon would I want to move in. I paged Rudy and I told him what I had been doing to rent the house. I told him that I would call him the next day after I had finalized all of these arrangements with my newest landlord. Rudy mentioned I should get also get ready to come out to New Jersey in the next week. I managed to rent the house over the phone and Rudy took it from there. I flew back to New Jersey. I had arranged to meet Rudy at the same diner that we had used the first time. I got to Newark and rented a car at the airport counter and drove to my appointment. Rudy was already seated and waiting for me. He kissed me quickly and got right down to business. First, he wanted me to go out and rent out three different storage units. He gave me directions to a Kinko's where we would meet the next morning. Rudy said he was going to give me a crash course on using Macintosh computers. He also mentioned I was going to be taking a quick trip to Arizona in a few days. I should go ahead and get a room, and he would try to stop by or call me first thing in the morning. Rudy handed me another fake New Jersey driver's license for my use. I was already getting used to this and starting to expect things to be a certain way, like . . . very nice, comfortable and pampering to me. I felt like I deserved to be treated in a certain way and I was expecting it, now. The next morning I got to Kinko's at a few minutes after ten. I scanned the place but Rudy was not there yet. So I went ahead and sat down at one of the terminals and logged on. Rudy came in and sat down next to me. He had brought a disk with him and he stuck it in the computer. I started to take some notes on what he was telling me for future reference. Rudy clicked on to a category on his disk called "DL." I could see that it was for making drivers licenses. Rudy gave me a disk of my own that he said that he had copied from his own, and it was for me to keep and use. That morning we were working on men's licenses, the ones that I would be using to rent the storage units. I left Rudy and drove back to my hotel room. I started calling around to find the three storage places that I needed. I got dressed in my Kimmy get-up and went to each one, paying for three months of rent on each unit up front. At each location, I showed the person at the desk the photocopied driver's license that I was using for that particular unit and signed whatever name I was using on the forms they gave me to fill out.

I peeled out of my Kimmy guise and became me again. Rudy knocked on the door about two hours later. He grabbed me up and threw me down on the bed, kissing me. We made out for awhile on the bed. After a bit it was back to business. He needed me to get a cellular phone for him as soon as possible. Rudy said, while I was at it, I should also buy a second one that would be for Joe and I to use. From here on out, if anyone asked who I was, my new name was Maryann. All I thought was, can't we pick a cooler name than Maryann? He tells me that I am going to start transporting large sums of money for him, from New Jersey to Arizona, several times a month. I wanted to know what kind of risk factor I was dealing with here. Rudy smiled at me and assured me that the way that the money was packed up, it was virtually undetectable to the x-ray machine at the airports. He told me he himself had done it hundreds of times. I called Joe. I told him that I was about to fly with a bunch of money to Phoenix. Joe was a bit concerned. I assured him as Rudy had me, that it was safe and that it had been done hundreds of times. For some reason I was not the least bit concerned about the risks I was taking. Rudy had told me I would be paid anywhere from $1000 – 3000 per trip, depending on how much money I was transporting. He told me to pack a light bag, just to look legit, and to be at the airport in an hour. He had booked me on a flight to Phoenix and arranged for the people that were to receive the money to meet me outside the airline terminal. Rudy told me that I would give them the money and turn around and get right back on another flight that would take me back to New Jersey. When the plane touched down on the runway at the airport in Phoenix, it was around 10:00 at night. I disembarked with my luggage which, incidentally, I had not let out of my sight, and made my way outside. I waited by the curb for my new "friends" to arrive. Within about five minutes, a tan-colored Land Cruiser made its way in front of me. The lady in the passenger seat rolled down the window and asked me if I was Maryann. I affirmed that I was. She opened the back door and asked me to get in. I put the suitcase with money in the car and we drove around the airport once. I got out back where we had started out and said farewell. I went back into the airport and boarded my return flight. It seemed that every time I accomplished something for Rudy, he entrusted me with more responsibility immediately after. After such a short time knowing him, I had already moved more money for him than I had ever seen in my life.

I learned from Rudy that this money was all profits from marijuana distribution in the New Jersey/New York area. It went to Tucson, where Randy and his people would bring it across the border and into Mexico. There was a guy down there named Billy, and he was the head of this whole organization. As I understood it, Billy and Sid had been the heads over this giant, nation-wide marijuana distribution network, when they had had a violent disagreement over a drug transaction. Billy had accused Sid of ripping him off and they had split up. Rudy had been involved with both of them in this network. When Rudy had gotten arrested in Texas, Sid had decided that he could no longer trust him and had stopped working with him. So, technically, Rudy was working for Billy and Sid was running his own organization now.

The guy who ran the distribution business in the New York area was called Stretch. He was the one who collected all of these profits and gave them to Rudy, so that Rudy could arrange to get the money to Randy in Arizona. Basically, what Rudy did was coordinate all of the varied people's efforts and get not only the money out of the country to Billy, but also to make the arrangements that enabled the enormous quantities of marijuana to get from Mexico and into the New Jersey/New York areas.

This is really where I became valuable to the "company." I was to become, for the short period of time that I was involved, basically the one who would "front" this illegal operation with various legitimate seeming businesses, and personas. Rudy would take me step by step into helping him to organize and run this whole network. Not to say that I was not always little more than support staff, but the support that I was to give would enable things to continue to flow, as well as grow. In all things pertaining to this organization, Rudy was my mentor and boss. He taught me everything. After a while, Joe and I were doing many things on our own, at Rudy's directive.

Once I arrived back in New Jersey, I went right to my hotel and slept for almost twelve hours. Rudy had not mentioned anything about the duration of my stay, just that Joe was coming out soon. When I inquired as to how much longer he thought that I would be out here, he was very vague. I figured I would not worry about it, and instead should concentrate on the business at hand. Like a new place to stay. At the time, I still thought that it was pretty cool to be living in hotels. I was looking for a decent place, but nothing too swanky, as I had noticed that in staying in a real nice hotel, you became too noticeable, and I was looking to be low-key. I settled on a place on Route 1. Once ensconced, I paged Rudy to let him know where I was. He said that he wanted to come by and fool around before I went to pick Joe up. That was the first time that I actually had sex with Rudy. He liked somewhat rough sex. I could get into playing some of these games with him. I was willing to try anything sexual at least once. The main thing that bothered me was the fact that he wanted us to have an affair; Rudy did not want me to tell Joe about what we were doing together. To me, that wasn't part of the deal that Joe had kind of made with Rudy. I was also very uncomfortable keeping secrets from Joe, and having to lie to him if he came out and asked me if I was sleeping with our boss. I was also very intent on pleasing this guy and securing his approval and I could see that he was really into this. With each new piece of business that I took care of or transacted, my confidence in my abilities grew to the point where I felt quite untouchable. I also felt more alive then I had ever been, taking these big risks and trusting completely that I would sail through, and get away with anything I wanted. This attitude led to my downfall.

I went to get Joe. Rudy said that he was coming back with money, and all the equipment that was required to package it in preparation for my trip back to Arizona. I was very curious to see how this was done. Joe and I took this opportunity to smoke some pot together. It's funny, but for a big time marijuana trafficker, Rudy was against doing drugs of any kind. He was not thrilled that Joe and I got high.

Some time later, Rudy returned, lugging a big suitcase and a vacuum pump. He went back to his car and returned with the same type of overnight bag that I had used previously and a box. Once we were locked up in our room, he opened the suitcase and told us that there was over $500,000 in it, which we would count and then we would take out about 75 grand for expenses and paychecks. He wrote down the total that he was sending with me to Randy. Rudy would leave all the supplies with us, since we would be doing the packaging job ourselves, now. He said that he would watch us do it the next time to make sure we had it down, but after that, unless there was some kind of situation, it was our responsibility. I left for the airport about an hour after we were finished packaging up the money.

Once I arrived in Phoenix, I rented a car at one of the counters at the airport. I started on the long drive down to Tucson. I met Randy; all went well. I said good-bye and made the trip back to Phoenix. I was very tired. I found a cheap motel and went right to sleep, remembering to set the alarm so that I would not blow it and miss my flight to New Jersey. I had told Joe when I would be returning, so he was there to meet me when I arrived. I kissed him and told him that everything had gone great. It was already getting dark and I felt disoriented by flying so much and the time changes.

No rest for the wicked; Rudy continued to use me, Joe . . . always escalating. We were indispensable yet totally dependent. We actually formed a company, "partnering" ourselves with Rudy, considering the amount of leased space and real estate we were financially sharing. I was taking the transport risk, Joe had his own risks to deal with . . . so we became more vocal. It was fine with Rudy. So long as money was made. The temptations in this "life" were still winning any battles of conscience.

It was only when we found out that Randy was skimming that life changed. I don't know what happened to Randy; he "disappeared."

We tried to keep things running, we had so much going on, so much at stake. Paranoia was easy to cover with all the work to be done, the money and the stuff it bought. But I think we both knew, Joe and I, the gig was up. We were taking chances with anyone and everyone imaginable — how big did we really think we were? Soon enough, Rudy was in jail.

Then while I was away working in California, they picked up Joe too. Everything had fallen apart. Rudy and I hadn't been together in months, and at this point Caroline, his girlfriend, and I were all alone, hanging in the wind. Caroline was someone who would help, right? I paged Caroline to call the pay phone at a motel I was shacked up at. When she called me back, I haltingly told her all what I had come home to, up to and including the fact that I had been paging Joe that entire day before and that he was most likely in jail. I had no money and, apparently, I was on the run from the cops and the FBI. Would she help me out? I needed some money, by the way, Rudy owes me over sixty grand, and what should I do? Was there any way to bail Joe out of jail? Maybe we could flee the country and live in Mexico or something. I admit that my thinking was quite irrational, but I was in a total state of panic by now and I had no idea what to do. Caroline couldn't believe what I was telling her any more than I could. She told me to sit tight, to stay out of sight and she would talk to Rudy when he called her. She would page me when she could. I should do nothing until I had talked to her first. I told her that as I had a lot of incriminating things with me, I was going to destroy these things. What they already had on us was bad enough. She agreed with me and reiterated that I needed to try and stay calm and stay inside my room. I told her where I was, and we hung up. I felt a little better after talking to her, but the panicked feeling that was coursing through me needed a hell of a lot more than what she had given me. I figured Rudy would know what to do, and I went back to the room.

I rolled myself a couple of fat joints and sat down and smoked them both. That done, I was a bit calmer and I opened up my luggage and started going through what I had. There were lots of papers, including the last few weeks of ledgers that I had concerning money coming in and expenses. I started tearing up all of these papers into little pieces and flushing them down the toilet. Once I had gotten rid of all of the papers, I made a pile of things that I wanted to get rid of that could not be flushed away. I had the wig that I had been using to rent places in Tucson and California, as well as three different pagers. I decided to keep only the one pager that I knew Caroline had the number to. I had the keys to a couple of PO boxes and my computer disc that had all the information on it that I used to make false driver's licenses and all other phony documentation. Obviously, the cops had figured that all of this kind of information was on the computer at the house, but they were wrong on that one: it was all here on this disk. They would find nada on the computer itself. But the files that they had taken from my desk were enough to send me to prison for years. I could not do anything about that now, except worry about it.

I smoked some more pot to take my mind off it. Then I took this little bundle of stuff out of the room and made my way to the back of the motel where there were some dumpsters. I threw everything into one of the dumpsters and went back into my room. All I could do now was to wait for Caroline's call. I decided that I needed a shower, as it had been awhile since my last one. I was tired and grubby and the shower was divine. I was so worried about Joe though. I was freaking myself out. I continued to smoke pot, and since it was such weak stuff I was barely feeling it. I finally felt good enough to lay down on the lumpy bed and try to take a little nap. I knew that I needed some sleep to think clearly and figure out what I was going to do now.

I woke up because my pager was going off. It was Caroline. It had been almost four hours since I had called her. She said that she was sorry it had taken her so long to get back to me but she had only just spoken with Rudy. We talked about getting this lawyer guy to go and see Joe and try to get him bailed out of jail. She couldn't be sure that anyone was looking for me, but most likely they were and if they found me, they would put me in jail too. I had to look out for myself and that would be the only way to be of help to Joe. We arranged to meet and Caroline picked me up. I got into her car with all of my stuff and we drove to a nice hotel. In the car she handed me $5500 and I checked into a room for a couple of days. She came with me to the room so that we could talk in private. I asked her if she had spoken with Rudy again and she said that she had. I guess that they had sent their lawyer over to speak with Joe and he had refused to see him! All I could do was wonder what on earth he was thinking.

Caroline said she did not really know what was going on, but the attorney had told her that Joe was being held on a quarter of million dollar bond, and that there was no way that we could bail him out. Without a lawyer to speak to the judge or prosecutor, there was also no hope of getting his bail amount reduced. The lawyer told Caroline that he thought that they could flush me out by holding Joe for so much money.

I was thinking unreasonably again, saying that I should try to see him and talk to him. She said that I was being stupid, they would find out it was me and I would be locked up as well. I said okay, you're right, but I am freaking out here. She said she understood, because she still did not understand what the hell Rudy was still doing in jail either. I told her that this whole situation was going down the tubes and I was really uncomfortable sticking around in New Jersey. I did not have a car, since I learned that when Joe had been arrested, he was going into a bagel shop and they busted him getting out of the car and seized it. Could she possible get me a one-way ticket out?? She said she could do that for me. I could leave the next day and drive back. I would stay in touch with her along the way, so that she could tell me if there was any news that I needed to know about. I hugged her and thanked her for all of her help, saying that I honestly did not know what I would do without her. She said that maybe another person who might be of some help was Billy. She had his pager number and had spoken to him a few times about the situation with Rudy. She said that he was aware of everything I had done and would probably help me out in some way, especially to keep me out of jail. I took the number. She did say, though, that Billy was not aware of the fact that so many people in the East Coast end of the network had been picked up. That was when she told me that Stretch had been arrested too, as well as a lot of the people who worked for him in New York. Then she also broke down and informed me that the lawyer had learned that the FBI and the state cops were also aware of the location of the warehouse and had searched it the same day that they did our house.

Well, it did not take a genius to figure out that we had obviously been under surveillance for at least a month or so. I wondered what else they knew. Caroline left to grab a ticket for my flight out to LA. At that point, I really did not know what else to do. I also had to hope that they weren't following Caroline around. I mean, why would they wait? She came back about an hour and a half later with my ticket for a flight the next morning. I could take a cab to the airport and drive back in my car.

First of all, I had to assume I was a fugitive from justice, that there was a warrant out for my arrest. They knew who I really was, and I had to go underground. I did not have any fake ID's to use. Once I was in California, I was tempted to seek out my sister and have her hide me out there or something, but I could not put her or her family into jeopardy. So I couldn't stay in California. I bought a map of the United States and went into a place to eat and figure out the best route back. I was so scared for Joe and I was missing him so terribly. I would break into tears if I thought about all of this too much and I really tried not to think about what was going to become of me or how Joe was holding up being locked up in a jail cell. I wondered if I should turn myself in, or maybe instead of going back east, I should just head south and into Mexico, or maybe head north into Canada. I decided to do what I had intended to do in the first place and drive back towards the east. I wanted to at least be near Joe.

At least, that is what I told myself. I was still thinking that there had to be some way to get him out of jail. I arrived in Pennsylvania after midnight. I pulled my tired self out of my car and limped into one of the hotels by the airport. I was dead to the world and giving them a fake name and paying in cash, I dragged myself into the room and collapsed on the bed, falling asleep instantly with all of my clothes on. After awhile, I paged Caroline to let her know that I had made it back okay. I had called her once or twice on my driving marathon across the country and there wasn't much news that was good to talk about. She was almost positive that there was a warrant out for my arrest, and there had been a couple of articles in the newspaper, mentioning Joe's arrest and that they were looking for me. Other bad news was that Rudy was still in jail and not getting out any time soon, if at all. It seemed that the feds had caught on awhile before to this scam that he had been running on them with his "cooperation" and they were pissed as hell. My money was dwindling and I did not think I could go on like this for more than a month. I could not believe that all of this had blown up in our faces.

Things took another type of turn when my pager went off while I was lying around in yet another hotel room. I was so surprised that I almost fell off of the bed. I looked at it and it was some weird number not in this area. I thought fast and dug in my purse for the number that Caroline had given me for Billy. It looked like the same type of number and I was instantly on my feet. Oh shit, what was he calling me for? What did he want?? I was quite nervous to call but I was more worried about what he might think if I did not. I had never spoken to him before and I did not know what to expect. He was very soft spoken, at least at first and asked about the troubles out here and why I hadn't asked for his help. I told him that I had not wanted to do that, that I was just laying low and trying to stay out of jail. Obviously, Caroline had still not really mentioned the severity of our problems out here and I decided that I would, since it would be stupid to try to lie to him. I said that everyone except me that I knew of was in jail and there was nothing that I could do about it; that the last thing that I had done was to get the warehouse in California, but that I could not go back there, as I assumed that the cops were probably crawling around everywhere. I had no idea if one or all of the people that had been arrested were talking to the feds and I could not risk the exposure. They were looking for me and had driven me out of the house I lived in. I told him that Rudy, Stretch and Roy (Joe) were all in jail and I was on the run.

He started freaking out about how he had to have the money that Rudy and Stretch owed him, how it was over $10 million and I had to somehow get it for him, because some people had kidnapped his partner because it was owed to them and all of this was Rudy's fault and what was I going to do to help him get his partner back? These people would kill him, unless they got all of this money. $10 million!? Over the next few days, I talked to Billy again. His partner was still missing and he was not sure that he was not already dead. At least this is what he was telling me. After I had gotten off the phone with him, I paged Caroline and told her that Billy was extremely agitated and wanted a hell of a lot of money that he said was owed to him. She flatly refused to talk to him and asked me if I could continue. I said that I would.

These calls were fairly depressing and I knew that sooner or later I was going to have to make a decision about what in hell I was going to do. Ironically, I was deciding what to do about my own problems when I heard about the whole OJ Simpson thing on the news. In fact, it was during the whole Bronco chase, down the freeways in LA that I knew so well, that I finally made the decision to contact my family and let them in on what was going on with me. These were bound to be extremely difficult phone calls to make and I had to mentally prepare myself to actually do this. As I watched OJ's Bronco being followed, I first called my father. I knew that he would be the most level-headed about this predicament. I was less emotionally involved with my dad than with my mother or sister and he could probably give me better advice for this particular problem. I was actually sympathizing with OJ, thinking that at this one moment in time, we had something in common; we were both on the run from the law.

My dad was living in Hawaii, on the island of Oahu. Just small talk for a couple of minutes. Knowing I really had to get to the point, I finally blurted out that I was in trouble. As calmly as I could, I explained to him what I had in fact been doing He made suggestions ranging from flying out to Hawaii and hiding out at his place to calling the FBI agent who had so kindly left his number for me when he searched my home. My dad also was upset with me for reasons that might be different than one imagined. He actually chastised me for not getting him involved in the deal, that if I had done so, things would have turned out differently! My dad is an unusual person to be sure, but this reaction was one that I did not really expect from him or anyone else. He finally advised that I should at least consult with an attorney and this lawyer could find out what was really going on for me. I found a guy named John Elbert who was licensed to practice in New Jersey and Pennsylvania. I called the number and got his answering service. I left my name and telephone number and told them that it was very important that he called me back as soon as possible. I paged Caroline and when she called back I told her that I was going to see a lawyer and explore the possibilities that were open to me. She sounded relieved and said she was also engaging an attorney to figure out what could be done in her case. She said she loved Rudy, but had to look out for herself. I agreed, and said that was pretty much my thinking of late too.

I drove away from his office after checking for a tail — not that I would have seen one if there was one, since I had no experience in that sort of thing, after all — and headed for my motel to grab my stuff and head for Maryland or Delaware. I had received the cash from my dad the day before and had at least a few days' worth of money. When my pager went off that night, I saw that Billy was trying to get me to call. I had too many problems of my own and I did not want to have to listen to any more of his. I ignored it and when it went off two or three more times in the next hour or so, I finally turned the damn thing off. I waited to hear from this lawyer, and when he called, I told him a little about what had happened and he said I needed to come to his office and discuss it in more depth. He said that it was unwise for me to say too much on the telephone. He was encouraging, and possibly even more paranoid than I was. I was extra careful driving to his office and practically snuck into the building. Once I got in the door, I was hustled into this guy's office and he told me to tell him everything about what I had been doing and what the feds could have on me. Once I had explained all of this he told me that he would handle my case with the feds, but he needed a retainer. I did not have much money anymore but that I could give about $2200 now and probably some more from my dad in a couple of days. I handed over practically every cent that I had. John (the lawyer) told me that he had handled this sort of thing before and I was in good hands. What a fairytale that turned out to be. He wasted no time telling me that I was looking at twenty years in prison and that he had discovered that there were all kinds of warrants out for my arrest. I asked him in a calm voice, (where it came from I don't know) what I could do to lessen that number of years behind bars. He said that it would be difficult, but that he would work out a proffer agreement and he would orchestrate the arrangements in the next week with all those concerned. John then asked me if I had ever thought about cooperating with these people, as it was practically the only way.

Eventually out of money, I had only this attorney to call . . . I had to have a place to go. I called him up from a pay phone and told him my plight, and asked him what should I do. He says I should come and stay with him at his apartment. John also mentioned the fact that most nights he himself did not stay there and that I would mainly be by myself. He added we were close to coming to a deal with the US attorney and there were things we needed to discuss, which we could do easier if I was at his place. I agreed. I had nowhere else to go. He would stay there that night and we could talk.

In the meantime, he urged me to start writing down the things that I remembered about the whole drug network that I had been working for. He wanted to be able to have my story about my role in everything to work with. I once again got my stuff together and retrieved the one night's worth of money that I would not be using for the motel room and with that $25 or so in my wallet, I headed back into Philadelphia.

It is hard and disturbing to me to attempt to describe what went on for the next five days or so, while I was staying at John Elbert's apartment. When I arrived, no one was there and I found a pad of paper and began to write some things down as he had directed me. After a couple of hours, John came home. That's when things started to get weird. He began popping pills that I would later find out were Prozac and Xanax, as well as drinking a lot of hard alcohol. All I could do was try not to show my shock at his decidedly unlawyer-like behavior. Then he stripped until he was completely naked and, turning on his VCR, began watching a hard-core porno flick. I was trying to believe that my whole existence was just a bad dream that I would eventually wake up from, and find Joe sleeping beside me.

I decided I had better find a way to deal with this freak until I surrendered to the feds. So as he sat there watching this video, he tells me that he wants me to take off my clothes too. I get up and start to grab my stuff and I say something like, I am going to leave, thanks anyway. Then he starts getting violent, telling me that I am nothing and without him I will go to prison forever. Then he calms down and asks me to please stay. I'm just standing there with my jaw dropping to the floor, wondering to myself what perverse stroke of fate brought me to this demented man. I felt like I was trying to awaken from this bad dream and without meaning to I pretty much dissolved onto the floor and, moaning Joe's name, I started weeping uncontrollably. He tells me to please stop sobbing and he will get the couch or something ready for me to sleep on, and if I still want to leave the next day, then that is fine, but I should get some sleep.

At this point I was freaked out beyond caring, so I dumbly nodded okay. And then he was back to being the pervert again. Finally he gets himself together and starts taking more pills and drinking. I'm trying hard not to look at him. I just want to get some sleep. Or die.

The next morning he was completely normal and he left for work without really saying anything to me. I tried to comfort myself with the fact that he had not tried to rape me and he was just eccentric. In the light of day, these things seemed more easily handled, but I was freaked just the same. I could not just rationalize it all away. John called later that day to see how I was doing, but just in general, not because of what he had put me through. He said that he wanted to take me out to dinner that night. We needed to talk about my case, and by the way, had I arranged to get him any more money yet from my father? I told him that I would call my dad. How much exactly did he need? He said something like ten grand. He said that he had to have the money before he would work anything out with the feds for me. I said, but I gave you over two thousand dollars already. I hung up the phone and wondered if I shouldn't just get out before something even more bizarre happened, but I was tired of running and hiding and I did not go. I was stuck in inertia, paralyzed. I was almost resigned to being tormented by him. I did not have the strength anymore to fight, or to leave the situation. I did call my dad and because I was embarrassed and ashamed of the predicament that I felt that I had put myself in, I did not tell him what the attorney had put me through the night before. I did tell him that he was letting me stay at his place for a little while and that he was asking if I could come up with some more money to pay for his services. I should have told my dad the truth and begged for his help, but I was so sick at heart. I just wanted this to be over. Anyway, my dad said it would take a couple of days to put together the money and he wanted to speak to this lawyer himself. I told him I would tell John and arrange for them to speak within the next day. The next couple of days were quiet and calm, since the attorney stayed away from the apart-ment. Then the fun and games started in again. This time when John came home, he brought his girlfriend with him. She was basically nice but, once the both of them began drinking, it got extremely weird. They were both getting real smashed and John was grabbing his pill bottles again and downing handfuls. Once he was good and messed up, he started harassing me about the money. When I got upset at this, he started telling me I should calm down and we could all have some fun. I kind of slunk away into the kitchen and slowly sipped a drink while I talked to Joe in my head.

I called my dad, and while we are speaking, John yells at my dad drunkenly, incoherently — and lurches at me and throws the phone. Now dad knows . . . I was basically hysterical at his behavior and he was really scaring me. John calmed himself and did his best to put on his lawyer mask and get me to stick around, saying that we had an appointment on the 28th of June in the US Attorney's office and that he would represent me there, even though I owed him money. He said that we could work it out later, but that he would do what he could to keep me out of jail. Then he promptly turned back into your average nut case and lunged at his girlfriend. I snuck off to find a corner to try to fall asleep in. I was due to go and surrender to the feds in only two days. It was all too much, and if I was going to jail in a couple of days, so be it. I was sick and tired of living this way and I was ready to do whatever I had to do to try to make this all go away. John and this woman were fighting now, screaming and ugly. She grabs me and tells John that we are going out.

We drove to the heart of Philadelphia and got out of the car and started walking down a busy street. We went past a bunch of stores and then she went into a video store and rented a few movies. Then we walked over to a place that she said had the best Philly steak sandwiches. They were great. I was feeling a lot better being out of that apartment. Being in the city was good for me too; I felt anonymous and free for the first time in awhile. She was kind of asking me questions about what I had done to be in so much trouble and I answered her with a very condensed version of only some of the stuff that had been going on with Joe and I. I did not know her and I realized that even though it would have been great to be able to really unload on someone about all the stuff that was going on and how I was feeling about it, I could not trust her with all of that. She was using the phone every couple of blocks and I asked her who she was trying to get a hold of. She looked me over like she was deciding how much she could trust me with. Then she told me that she was trying to call her dealer to score some coke. I was like, oh yeah, why didn't you tell me? I said that I would love to get high and what was going on? She hastily told me that she did not do a lot of the stuff, but every so often she was into it. Yeah, right. She asked me not to tell John and I told her that I had no reason to do that, since what she did was none of his business. She made another call and this time she got through to somebody and we walked back to the car and took off. She drove to a place and parked and told me to wait, that she would be right back. I knew the drill, no problem. She came back out in a couple of minutes and she drove to a place that she said was her apartment. We both went inside and after turning on a few lights and checking on the place, she took out the coke and started chopping it up and laying out some lines. I snorted what she gave me, enjoying the tickle in my nose and the drip in my throat, not to mention the instantaneous buzz that I got. She turned on some music and we snorted lines and talked about her relationship with John, and other relationships that she had had in the past. I told her all about Joe and how much I was missing him, that we were engaged to be married, and that he was all I could think about. I told her that I was grateful to John for his help, but that he was really messed up with alcohol and pills and I was real nervous about turning myself in with a lawyer like him. She reiterated that he was very good and that even though he was personally a wreck, which she agreed with, he would do a good job and I should trust him. I told her that he had personally put me through a new kind of hell the last week, but I guess I had no choice but to believe in him. She said that I seemed like a strong person and that I would get through this. It was nice to be talking to someone like this and I expressed to her that I really appreciated her kindness and was glad that I had met her. It was pretty late and we figured that John would be crashed out by now so we drove back to the apartment and crept inside. He was, in fact, out cold, and so we snorted some more lines and put in one of the movies that she had rented. We made drinks and commenced getting fairly wasted together. I was having a nice time, the best in quite awhile and I was sorry when she said that she had better get going, herself. I was really wired from the cocaine, and I knew that I would not be sleeping for awhile, but I said goodnight and she left.

I turned the TV back on and watched stupid show and wrote in my legal pad about how I had gotten involved with Danny, Sid and Rudy. I was filling the pad up and I was remembering things as I wrote. John had wanted something like this for himself and that it could be helpful with the feds, but I figured that they could get information out of me whether I wrote it down or not. If I was willing to give it to them.

I was still not sure if I should cooperate with them or not. It would go against everything that I thought I stood for to bend over now. I could not help but question myself, though; what did I really stand for, anyway? What did I believe in and whom was I loyal to? I needed this time to really ponder these questions and others like them to figure out not only what I was going to do once I was in a room with a bunch of cops and lawyers, but what did I really want for myself, now and in the long run? Better late than never to finally figure out that I needed to know these things for myself.

The next day was quiet after John went to work and my dad still would not speak with me. I called my mom to let her know what was happening and that I was due to surrender to the FBI the next morning and maybe she could get a message to dad, since the attorney that I had been staying with had really pissed him off and now he would not talk to me. She assured me that she would try to reach him and wished me luck, and asked would I please let her know as soon as I could what had happened, even if I was in jail, which we both knew was a real strong possibility. I felt better after talking to her and I was so relieved that she was on my side. I knew that she was very scared for me as well as extremely disappointed in me, but she was offering me her unconditional motherly love and support and I was immensely grateful and so glad that she was my mom.

I kind of loafed around for the rest of the day, walking down to the corner store once to get a bite to eat and then back to the legal pad to write some more stuff down. There was so much to write and I was barely even cracking the surface, even though I had written about fifteen pages so far. I knew that I was fighting a losing battle and so instead I just concentrated on psyching myself up for the next morning. I really did not know what to expect as I had never turned myself into the FBI before. What would happen to me? Was there really any way to help myself out by cooperating with them?? I just did not know. I would find out when I got there, and that was all I could do; be strong, brave and as true to myself as I could be. That night when John got home, for once he did not just start drinking, and we had a talk about what I could expect to happen the next day. He said that if I cooperated, there was a fairly good chance that I could walk out of there; but they could just as easily throw me in jail. It depended on lots of factors and we were going in there pretty blind, but that couldn't be helped. He said that it was good that I was going in there of my own free will, and that would certainly count for something. What kind of stuff I could tell them would also be a deciding factor in what they would do with me. John said that he had done this before and he was there primarily to protect me and my rights and that he would do whatever he could to help me. He was being so reasonable that I was struck by the difference of the calm, intelligent lawyer that I was talking to and the maniac that he could become in the blink of an eye.

John got up and made himself a drink and downed some pills and got comfortable on the couch, but so far his clothes were still on, so I tried to relax and not think too much about my situation there or what might happen to me the next day. Then his girlfriend showed up and the party started, at least for the two of them. It was more of the same and I just tried to ignore them as best I could. Of course, after a couple of hours and bottles later, they started fighting, screaming and swearing loudly at each other. What a relationship! I felt sorry for both of them, and since there was nothing that I could do, I just locked myself in the bathroom until the yelling stopped, which was quite awhile. I unlocked the door in time to see her storming off, but she stopped long enough to wish me luck the next day, which was very nice of her under the circumstances.

I did not want to be alone with John. He yelled at me to make him a drink and when I brought it out, he grabbed me and made me sit right next to him. Ugh. At least he did not try to touch me or anything, but I was so very uncomfortable and jail was beginning to look appealing to me. After a bit, I was able to get away from him, saying that I needed to get some sleep. I curled up in my usual corner and did not wake up until the next morning.

I was up early, mostly due to my extreme nervousness regarding what I was about to do. I was ready to go and I had not even heard John stirring once. I yelled up at him to get up, that we had to leave. He was not even awake!! I finally heard him groaning and getting into the shower. I fidgeted around for another hour or so when he finally came downstairs, asking me if I was ready to go. I fought to keep a rude remark from coming out of my mouth and said sure, let's get this over with. Little did I know that the fun was just beginning for me. It was a long drive to Newark from Philadelphia and on the way John stopped to get something to eat. I wasn't hungry and my stomach was already a nervous mess, but I sipped a coke and he told me not to be worried, that everything would be fine. Easy for him to say, since he wasn't the one who was going to be in jail by the end of the day. He told me that I did not know that, so I should think positively. That was true enough, and so I just sat quietly while he finished eating. We got back on the turnpike and before I knew it, we were at the Federal Building and I was walking inside to my destiny. We went up the elevator to the floor where the US attorney's office was located. They made us wait quite awhile, which was probably because we were late and they had been waiting for us to show up. I was just hoping that they would even see us, at that point. I kept waiting for a guard to come out, handcuff me, and lead me away. I was so nervous.

At last, the door opened up and a guy came out and told us to come in. He led us into a large conference room where there was already a roomful of people sitting at the table. As soon as we were asked to be seated, a handful of the people left the room and there were only three other men there besides John and I. They were introduced to me as Mr. McKenna, the assistant US attorney; Mr. Wilkes, the FBI agent in charge of our case; and a guy named Mr. Palka, who represented the criminal division of the IRS. Sometime between the wait in the lobby and sitting in front of these law enforcement people, I had made the decision that I was going to do whatever I had to do to save myself from twenty years in prison. I was going to tell them everything and do anything that I had to do to lessen my sentence. I was going to be loyal to myself and also to Joe, whom I had decided I would talk about, but I would state up front that I would never testify against him for any reason.

They wanted me first to tell them as much as I could about everything from the beginning of my involvement with my illegal activities. It seemed to me that they only thing that they were not aware of was the cocaine shipment. They were caught of guard when I began talking about it, and got pretty excited at what I was telling them. Every so often as I was talking, one of them would ask me a question about this or that, or had I every heard the name so-and-so, and things like that. For the most part, though, they just let me talk, and all of them were taking notes the whole time. This interview went on for at least four hours and once I was finally done talking, I was drained and was apprehensive about what was going to happen next.

While these happy thoughts were going through my mind, they looked at me and asked me how much I was willing to do to help them out, and myself as well. I told them that I was essentially willing to do anything they asked me to do that might help us all. They said that they could not guarantee anything to me, but that if I cooperated fully, and performed what they called proactive work for them, they would go to bat for me at my sentencing. They started asking me detailed questions about Billy, and did I think that he would call me if I tried to reach him? I told them that he was probably miffed at me for not calling him the last time that he had been trying to reach me, and that it might take me awhile to get through to him, but that yes, I did believe that he would speak to me. They then inquired if I would be willing to tape record conversations with Billy. I said that of course I would do that. I told them honestly that I owed nothing to him and in fact he owed me a lot of money that I would of course never see. He did not mean anything to me and I would be happy to play along. I did have the presence of mind to ask how risky this was to me. They told me that they would be involved closely with me and that the risk was small at this point. As far as we knew, Billy had no idea what my real name was and certainly did not know that I would be cooperating with the feds. I would have to act convincingly, which I knew that I could do quite well, and get him to trust me again, after over a month-long absence. I told them that I still had one of my pagers and Billy would recognize the east coast numbers if I called him. He knew my code, which was "444," and would most likely respond eventually to my pages. They asked me if I had anything other than the evidence that they had already seized from the house when they searched it and I again truthfully told them that after I had discovered that Joe was in jail, I had destroyed anything that I had that I thought was incriminating to myself, but that there might still be something left at the house that they did not take, if I could go back there and look for them. Then they greatly surprised and gladdened me by telling me that I could in fact return to the Princeton house that Joe and I had shared, and could continue living there!! I could not believe that they were letting me go home, and I was practically in tears from my relief and shock. They fired out some more questions about portions of what I had told them and then kind of looked at me and asked me where I kept the rest of my money, that they knew that I must have at least several hundred thousand dollars stashed somewhere and they needed me to tell them where it was. I was incredulous that this was to be the point that they were so interested in and I frankly told them that they were mistaken, that the almost $51,000 that they had taken from our home in Princeton was all the money that we had. I explained that both Joe and I were owed money from the network, that we had not been paid for the last several months and that if we had been paid, there would be close to a million dollars. This point would continue to come up for the next four or five interviews that I was to have with these guys and others, and it took me quite awhile to convince them of this fact. They just could not believe that I was flat broke! Well, neither could I, but the truth is the truth and I stuck to the facts. It later came out that almost everyone in this organization had been skimming money and they were unbelieving when I stated that neither Joe nor I had ever done such a thing. We might have been outlaws, but we were never thieves. I held my breath, waiting for someone from the jail to show up and for them to tell me thanks, but we are putting you in jail.

They told me that they were finished for today, but they wanted me to go to a different location the next day to answer more questions. No problem, since I was floating on a cloud in my release from my anxieties about going to jail. John and I left, and I realized that he had not spoken a word since we had signed the proffer agreement over four hours ago. It also dawned on me that I had done most of this by myself, other than his getting this written agreement in the first place. I had not decided then, but it was in the front of my mind that I was going to unload this guy and he sure as hell had gotten all the money from me that he was going to get. We drove back to Philadelphia; my things were waiting packed and ready in his apartment. My car had been parked in a garage across the street and I thought that I had just enough money to pay for the parking fee. I thanked John for his help and his generosity in letting me stay in his apartment, even though in my heart I hated him for putting me through hell. I never wanted to see the rater again, and I never did.

Not that getting rid of him was going to be easy. I did not know that, then, though, and it was in a very lighthearted mood that I bid him farewell and drove my trusty car back into New Jersey and home to Princeton. Was it great to be back in my house or what?? I could not help saying to myself, and I searched through some stuff myself, hoping that I had somehow hidden some more money somewhere. No such luck. I checked out if there was any more weed left anywhere either and I came up dry on that count too. Looking around after I had tidied up, I knew that I would have to sell some of the things in the place, just to have enough money to live there and eat. I ate in front of the TV, back in the house that I never really expected to see again. I called my mom right away. She was very relieved that I was not in jail, and was helping the police so I would be out for awhile, and she promised to send me a little money until I had some things sold. I asked her to get a hold of dad for me and to tell him that I was going to blow off that horrible lawyer; that he was a freak; and I would tell her all about it some other time. When we hung up after saying I love you, I was feeling almost back to normal again. I slept better that first night than I had for at least a month. It was fine to be home, and to have a new lease on life, with a purpose and goals.

The next morning I got up and drove out to the next meeting that the feds had scheduled. This time, in addition to the FBI and IRS guys, there was a detective from the Somerset County prosecutor's office present for the questioning. The FBI guy wanted to talk more about the cocaine shipment that I had shocked them with the previous day. So I went into the start of the whole deal from when Rudy came back from Mexico after meeting with Billy. They had lots of questions about this, like who rented the room, where was it, stuff like that. I told them in greater detail exactly what Billy had told Rudy about the cocaine shipments, and what Joe and I would have to do to make it happen. Not that Billy knew us, he just knew that Rudy had people that performed these functions for him and that in a nutshell was what made Rudy a large player, and a valuable person to a guy like Billy. If Billy knew that there was no great mystery to getting these places and realized that almost anyone could do it, he would have no use for a man like Rudy, and Rudy knew this, so he always played these kinds of things up to Billy like he was accomplishing the impossible on a daily basis. I also elaborated on others that I had known or been aware of within the organization itself.

They then told me that the interview was over for the day, but that the detective from Somerset County wanted to interview me at length about the scam that Rudy had set up for the turning in of planted evidence, like pot and large amounts of cash, so that he could turn these things in himself and pretend cooperation. That took another couple of hours and then the FBI agent came back in and told me that I could go home, but that he and the IRS guy would be stopping by the house in a couple of days to go over what kinds of things they wanted me to do to help them with their continuing investigation of this whole network. Before I left, I asked them about Joe, who had been heavily on my mind. They were willing to tell me that they were also talking to him and that he was cooperating with them too. That eased my mind somewhat, and so I decided that I had nothing to lose, and inquired if it would be possible for me to talk to him. He said that he did not see any problem with that and he then promised that he would make sure that word got to Joe that I was at the house in Princeton and that it was okay to call me. I was so happy to hear that!! I thanked him profusely and tearfully. I did not know how soon Joe would call me, but there was no way that I wanted to miss his call, not after so long. I was simply dying to hear his voice, to know that he was all right, to tell him that I loved him and missed him terribly. I also thought that if they would let us communicate by phone, that they might not be adverse to a more personal meeting, like my being allowed to go to the jail and see him there. I was more excited and hopeful than I had been in awhile and it was in this more optimistic mood that I drove toward home.

I made some calls to find out how to go about getting a public defender. I had to fire John. There had been a message on my voice mail at home from him, wondering when he was going to get more money. I would rot before he would see another penny from me. I called him and told him that I was retaining a public defender and that his services were no longer required. He freaked out, screaming and threatening me; he would make sure that I went to jail forever, he would do this, he would do that . . . I remained calm, however, in the face of his ridiculous threats, even though part of me was a bit fearful. He was pretty much out of control and unpredictable; maybe he would really try to hurt me. He did know where I was living, that I was alone and vulnerable.

The phone rang and I went to answer it, thinking that maybe it was Joe. It was John's girlfriend, and although she started the conversation normally enough, it was soon obvious that she was on his side. Before I knew it, while I was simply attempting to explain my side of things and why I felt the way I did about John, she began shrieking and threatening that she knew things about my case that she could use against me. That she could really make life even rougher for me and I had better pay John the money that I owed him before they both drove over to my house and took care of me but good. I did the only thing that I could, which was to tell her to go to hell, and I hung up. I was shaking; I was so furious with these people. Didn't I have enough nonsense going on without these crazy scummy people threatening me? Of course, the phone rings again almost immediately, and I reluctantly answer it, hearing this bitch scream how I should never hang up on her, and I would be sorry that I had. I said, listen, I have nothing more to say to you or John, why don't you get a life and leave me alone? I listen to her yelling abusive stuff at me and then she again threatens me, saying that they knew where I was and they would come over and cut me up or something worse. I did not appreciate being threatened in this manner and I was sick to death at this point of these dreadful people. I said, oh really, we'll see if you and your pervert boyfriend have the balls to do that. I slammed the phone down and called the police.

They did not know this, but the feds had already given me this portable tape recorder that I would be using to tape conversations with Billy and whomever else I could get to call me. I had taped the threatening conversations with not only John, but his whore of a girlfriend as well. I told the police that I was being threatened and by whom, telling him what kind of car John drove and that he was my ex-attorney. The police told me that they would drive by my house for the next week or so on an hourly basis, and if I received any more of these threats, I should let them know. Once I arrived back at the house, the voice mail service had a couple of new messages. They were more threats from John's girlfriend, with John in the background. I saved the messages so that I could play them for the police later and I got ready to get through the night. I got a sharp knife out of the kitchen and prepared to use it if these idiots thought they were going to try to enter my home and hurt me, or even scare me. I was as mad as I had been for a long time.

I also made a phone call to the FBI agent. I informed him of what had taken place and the fact that I had called the local police for protection. He was also concerned about my safety and I told him that I was prepared to defend myself if I had to and that the cops were going to cruise my house throughout the evening. He told me to please call him if anything at all came up and I assured him that I would. These stupid people had no idea whom they were dealing with. I had to smile when I thought of the reaction that the police must have gotten when they contacted John about my complaint and played him the tapes that I had made. I had had it with people thinking they could intimidate me or harass me. Those days were over with for me. It was the first time in my life that I had ever called the cops for anything.

Since I was out of money again, I put an ad in the paper to sell my stair-climber machine, which was in excellent condition. I also played my beautiful red guitar for the last time and put it and my amplifier in the trunk of my car and drove to the place I had purchased them from. I received about $500 for the both of them. One night that wonderful week, the phone rang and when I picked it up, I heard my beloved Joe saying, "Cuddles, is that you?" I was so overjoyed to hear from him that I was in tears.

Actually, first I heard the operator asking me if I would accept a collect call from the Somerset county jail, but that part was blurred in my recollection. I found out that he was doing okay, even though there was no hope in hell of his getting released in the near future. I tried to be cheerful, and told him that the agents had told me that sometime soon I would be allowed to come and see him. It was a happy but sad conversation, all at the same time. It was so fine to talk to him again, but very hard to just talk to him when I desperately needed him with me, and knowing that was impossible. Before I knew it, his fifteen minutes on the phone were up and we said an emotional good-bye. He did manage to tell me before the phone disconnected that he would call the next night at around the same time, which I was thrilled to hear. I felt such bittersweet emotions after I hung up the phone, loving him so much and missing him, needing him with me, especially now. I had to get a grip on myself and stay strong, but it was so hard to do.

A couple of days later, the FBI agent and the IRS guy showed up at the house as promised. We tried to get Billy to call me, without success. I pointed out to them that most likely Billy was a bit irritated at me for basically ignoring him when he had been trying to get a hold of me a few weeks back and would definitely make me sweat a bit before he finally called me back. He would probably only call me when he got curious enough. I was the only one who could do the things that could get him back in business again, and once he thought about it, he would call. We would all have to be patient until that happened. These guys just smiled at that, and I had to laugh and tell them that of course I knew that they were very patient and had nothing else to do but wait, like me. I told them that I would try on my own at night, and like they did, I would travel far enough away from my house, so that in case he had some way of tracing the call, he could not be sure where I was really staying. When Joe called me later that night, I told him a little about what I was attempting to do and that so far Billy had not called me back, but that I was certain that within a week or so he would. Joe was worried that I was putting myself in a potentially dangerous position, and I tried to allay his fears by saying that the feds were monitoring all of this stuff and I was pretty safe. Too soon, our time was up and he told me to be at home the next night at the same time, he would call back. I always felt so lonely after getting off the phone with him, but strengthened in a way, too. I thought that I felt bad; I could not even yet imagine what Joe had to go back to.

At least that screwy lawyer John and his girlfriend had stopped harassing me and I was going to get a public defender the next day. My family was being supportive and I felt very lucky to be on the outside and not inside a cell like Joe was. I was going to make the most out of this chance that I had been given to do the right thing after doing the wrong stuff for so long. I met with my new lawyer the next afternoon. Her name was Tonianne Bongiovanni and I liked her from the start. She was glad that I was fully cooperating with the feds and told me that she would be able to help me since I was doing all I could to assist in the ongoing investigation. She told me about possible plea bargains that we might accept and things like a 5K1.1 motion that could be filed in my behalf that could reduce my sentence by fifty percent. All in all, it was a good meeting and I felt comfortable with her high level of competency and the fact that she was on my side and would help me with getting my sentence lowered as much as it realistically could be.

That night when Joe called me, he began telling me some things about this guy that he had met in jail. He said that his name was Richie and he was a great guy and that he was very knowledgeable about a lot of legal stuff and he wanted to help us out. I was naturally skeptical, but Joe assured me that this person was for real and that he was going to put him in touch with me and that I should listen to him, do whatever he said that I should do; and then Joe said that even if it came down to me marrying this man, that I should do it! I'm like, what the hell are you talking about? I told Joe that I was not about to marry anyone but him under any circumstances, how could he even say such a thing? Joe said, okay, maybe that was a bit extreme, but that I should not count it out, that if it could help me in some way, I should at least consider it. I thought that jail was making Joe really crack up. I couldn't believe that he was saying these things and that I was supposed to take them seriously. Joe said that this Richie was helping him out in jail and that he could do things to help me out too. I told Joe that I was not sure that I wanted to talk to this guy. Joe said that I could trust him and again he stated that Richie could really do things for me. Joe said that he was more concerned with helping me and keeping me out of jail than he was with himself. I told him that I was completely cooperating with the feds and that was what had kept me out of jail. Joe said that Richie could keep me out of jail permanently if I did what he said. I told Joe that I loved him and appreciated what he was saying, but that I was sick of putting my trust in people who were messed up. I told him a little bit about my attorney experience just so that he would understand where I was coming from. As I had feared, Joe was greatly upset by even the small details that I gave him about that awful time, and he asked me why I had not told him this before. Because it would upset you, like you are now, and there was nothing that you could do about it, right? He said that I was right, but he still did not want me to keep things from him, no matter what. On that note, our time was up and I asked Joe if he could call the next night, we could talk about this some more. We said our lonely but loving good-byes and I hung up the phone. I had continued to page Billy nightly and so far I had not gotten a return call. I had expected this, though, and I was still positive that it was only a matter of time. I was talking to Joe almost every night and one night right after our conversation regarding Richie, he told me that he had not wanted to tell me something, but that I should know that he had seen Rudy in the jail and that Rudy had tried to hurt him. I freaked out and was practically screaming that he needed to tell me exactly what had happened.

He was real subdued and since he had caught me off guard, I was kind of at a loss as to what to actually say to him, now that he was actually calling me. Then the words just came pouring out. I apologized to him first of all for not returning his calls weeks back. I told him that I had been a total wreck and had just needed to disappear for awhile to figure things out. I said that I was still a fugitive and that my stash of money was running out and basically I needed to know where things stood with the business. Like, what was going on? This was when he dropped his mellow tone and got angry, with me, with Rudy, Stretch and just about everybody. Billy ranted and raved for at least fifteen minutes, sometimes incoherently, and I knew that I had to listen to him and let him get all of this shit out of his system. He was getting threatening with me as well, bitching at me that I had let him down by not calling for so long. He indicated that I could be killed too, and that I had better not be fooling around with him. Then he scared me again by asking me how it was that I was not in jail and how did he know that I was not working for the cops or something? I was putting on a sensational act by now, though, and I was actually able to convince myself and therefore him, that I would rather be dead than have anything to do with the police, whom I told him I utterly and completely despised. Which up until about two or three weeks ago, I certainly had. I guess that Rudy had gotten word that Joe had been talking to the feds that came around and had paid off some tough guys in the place to rough Joe up, Joe had to fight some guys that Rudy sent to beat him up and then after that episode Rudy had seen him and had threatened to kill him or something. If I had ever doubted that what I was doing was the right thing, after hearing this about Rudy, all my doubts were gone. Joe was okay and that was what mattered. He said that this Richie had helped him out with Rudy's "friends." I was still uncertain about this guy, but Joe again assured me that he was someone that we could trust and that he would be calling me the next night. I said okay, I would talk to him and if he could help out in some way, I would consider it. I had to wonder though, how much could another guy who was stuck in jail possibly help me? The next evening I went out again to attempt to reach Billy in Mexico. I had the monitoring equipment all set up and just as I was about to disconnect everything and call it a night, the phone rang. I was so surprised that I probably jumped about a foot. I answered the phone and turned the tape recorder on. It was Billy, and he was like, hey Maryann, what's going on?

I agreed with him that Rudy had double-crossed him, but I added that Rudy had screwed me too, and very much so. I told him that we needed to work together and not against each other, to make things work again. So by making our plight a common one, I calmed him down and got him talking much more rationally and finally getting him to agree that I was right. I patronized him without making it seem as though that was what I was doing and built up his ego by telling him that I was a hundred percent with him and that I would do anything that I could for him. By this time, I had kept him on the phone for almost an hour and I was thrilled that all of this was working out so well. Now that he was not pissed at me, we could angrily talk together about all of the other jerks who had let us down. He asked me about Roy, (Joe) and I told him that he was in jail too. I added that Roy had been royally screwed over by Rudy and that he was the only one of the whole crew that I had any ties to anymore. When this first conversation finally was winding down, I again told Billy that I was ready to work and that I would do whatever was necessary to help him, that he could reach me at anytime and I would be at his beck and call. I added that I was kind of working for some minor people in the business in the Philadelphia area that I had hooked up with and that was how I was getting by. I added that I had no loyalty to these people, however, and if he wanted me somewhere, I would be there. He seemed real happy with me by the end of this interesting talk, and he said that he was going to figure some stuff out and he would be in touch with me within a day or two. He ended up by telling me to be careful and take care of myself, and I offered the same back at him. After I hung up the phone, though, my state of mind was a very strange one. I alternated between feeling ecstatic that I had him trusting in me, and hating myself for betraying him. I could see that none of this was going to be easy for me, and that I would have to tread carefully between these two worlds that I was now in.

First thing the next morning, I paged the FBI guy that was in charge and when he called me back, I told him that I had gotten Billy on the phone the night before and I had a great tape for him to listen to. When the agents showed up, they took the tape and asked me what had happened. I explained in detail what we had talked about and told them that I should be hearing from Billy again within a couple of days. They told me that I was to contact them again the next time that I spoke with Billy and that they would be talking to me. I of course did not confide in them the war that was waging within me. I could not stand to see myself ratting out Billy and I could not reconcile myself to continuing, but I did not know what else I could do. Inside of me, I was so confused over where my loyalties should lie. I was real pissed at Rudy for many reasons, but what had Billy ever done to me? I was almost thinking that, for now, I would go along with the feds on all of this, but that if an opportunity came up for me to work with Billy again, that I could just take off and go to him in Mexico. I admit that these thoughts were very unorganized and not thought out whatsoever, but I was really at odds with what I was doing. I was truly an outlaw torn; I wanted to save myself but being an informer for the feds, the Authority that I had always distrusted and hated, was not coming easily for me and I really was loathing myself for selling out. I was an outlaw, even now to myself, and I felt that what I was doing was wrong. I would continue in a fashion to play both sides of the fence, since I was unresolved as to where I stood, with Billy and with the feds. My judgment was so messed up and I could not make a decision that I felt comfortable with.

That night I first got a call from Joe and then a few minutes after my fifteen minutes with him was up, Richie called me for the first time. I accepted the collect call and talked with him for awhile. He had a real Brooklyn-ese type accent, real New York tough. I found it kind of sexy, though. That was my mistake, believe me. My first instinct, though, was to never speak with him again, and to tell Joe that this guy was bad news and that we would deal with this mess ourselves. Somewhere in the back of my mind, I also thought that I could trust this guy if Joe said that I could. So even though he sounded just like some gangster out of a Mafia movie, I pretty much made up my mind to go ahead and befriend him. He did seem nice, and spoke well of Joe, at least at first. That would change, down the road, but for now, he really liked Joe. A lot of these early conversations are fuzzy to me now, but mainly it was small talk and eventually I learned that he had been in jail before, in fact he had served some thirteen years in prison all together. First, though, Joe had told him that I was working with the feds and I confided to him that I had made my first tape of a real heavy dude down in Mexico, a guy that the feds wanted really bad. He thought that this was great and before too long, he was telling me that he had in fact been let out of prison to set up some guys in one of the New York crime families. He had worn a wire and had sold them some guns and other stuff. He had been behind this huge bust and was getting ready to testify against the whole bunch in a couple of months and then he would be going into the federal witness protection program. Wow. Pretty heady stuff. He was totally encouraging me to do as much as I could for the feds and that it would only help me out. I told him that I had told the feds that whatever I was doing should also help Joe out. Richie said that that was fine, but I really had to think about myself first and Joe would do what he had to do for himself. He seemed to know a lot about the legal system and knew some technical things that only lawyers usually know. Richie said that he still had other cases up his sleeve, so to speak, and that he would only give these to the feds when they could be applied to my case and that way he could help me out. I was speechless; I asked him why he would do that for me, or Joe, for that matter. Richie said that he really liked Joe and after he had seen a picture of me that I had sent to Joe, he had thought that I was real cute and Joe had told him all about me and he wanted to help me out any way he could. I was suspicious of his motives, but I did not want to make him mad or anything. I mean, maybe he could do something to help us out. Richie added that, who knew, maybe I could marry him and come into the witness protection program with him. I kind of laughed and told him that there was no way that I could ever see that happening, but all he said was that I should give him a chance, something like that. I answered that I had a very open mind, but that was pretty farfetched. I was in love with Joe, engaged to marry him, and I did not see any way that that was going to change.

I had never met anyone like Richie before in my life and there was something about him that fascinated me and I was very intrigued by him. Almost how I felt about Rudy when I first met him, but this was even different than that. I still spoke lovingly to Joe almost every night, but something was changing and I would change with it, unfortunately. I was weak and Richie knew it; and he was going to take advantage of my vulnerability, even though I could not know it then. But he was very vulnerable as well and I cannot help but feel now that I should have seen so much more. Things were also progressing with my taped phone calls with Billy in Mexico. I was talking with him a couple of nights a week, and I was driving all over trying to make sure that he could never track me down to where I was really living. He was very gung-ho once he was over his initial suspicions about my reappearance in his life. One day when I went out to call him after he had paged me, I called his number and was I surprised when Randy answered the phone! You remember Randy, right? He was my guy down in Tucson, who had been fired right before all the trouble for us really started. I expressed my pleasure at talking with him again, and that he had evidently patched up his differences with Billy. He assured me that he had and that he was down at Billy's place to help put a new network together. He sounded totally drugged, and once Billy took the phone from him to talk to me, I could tell that he was quite wasted as well. It made me want to be with them down in Mexico, getting loaded and not having all of this terror hanging over my head. I spoke with Billy for awhile when all of a sudden I was at the end of the tape! Oh no! I continued the conversation since, I was having a good time talking to them, and I tried to keep in mind that I needed to try to remember everything that was said so I could relate the rest of the conversation to the feds. Randy jumped back on the phone and asked me what I was doing and I replied that I was laying low since the cops were after me. He told me that I should come down to Mexico and we could all talk about the future of our business together. I told Randy that at the moment I was almost flat broke and that I was afraid to attempt to fly out to see them, for fear that I could be apprehended, and that would be bad for all of us. He sympathized with my financial problems and offered to send me out a thousand bucks to tide me over for a couple of weeks. I explained to Randy that I had to go, but that if he could send the grand out Western Union, and he said sure, so we agreed upon a password that I could use to get the money so I would not have to show any identification. He was sounding even more loaded now than he had at the beginning of the conversation, but he stunned me by telling me that he loved me and that we would talk soon. I recovered somewhat from him saying that to me, and told him to let Billy know that I would be in touch in the next day or so. When I hung up the phone, I was feeling like a dirty piece of garbage again. This was so confusing!

I felt so torn again by all of this and I got into my car and tried to make sense of my messed up life and the conflicts that were raging away inside of me. As if I was not confused enough by what was going on with Billy, my personal life was getting out of control as well. Richie called me the next night and I was really glad to hear from him. Since he was also a "snitch," it was very good for me to talk to him about all of this stuff that I was doing. He was very encouraging and supportive; actually, forceful is a better way to describe it. He really pushed me to make contact with these people and make as many tapes of these conversations for the feds as I could. Every time I got some new piece of damning information recorded, he was so enthusiastic about what I was doing and that I should go right back out and get some more. On the other hand, Joe was not that interested in what I was doing, so I found myself more and more not really telling him what was going on. Richie was rapidly becoming someone who was very important in my life and Joe was growing less so. It was another area of my life that was very confusing to me. Then, out of the blue, as Richie and I were talking on the phone about more personal matters, something that we had just been starting to do all the time, he blurted out that he thought that he was falling in love with me. I was shocked that he would say such a thing and I quickly told him that that was ridiculous, that he barely knew me and that he was just lonely in jail. Richie said that I could think whatever I wanted to, but that he really was falling in love with me. What really terrified me was that I thought that I was falling in love with him, too. This was just too weird; I had never even met this guy and I was relying on him more and more everyday. He told me that he was going to send me a card or something in the mail and that he was going to include a picture of himself for me. I was interested in seeing what he looked like, that was for sure. We were starting to get very intimate with each other over the phone as well. Both of us were very sexual people and we were both starving for some kind of sex life. When you have nothing else, phone sex is okay. All of a sudden, it seemed like it was practically overnight to me, he was the center of my universe. How had this happened? Was I that much of a sucker for a few nice words and some understanding? It seemed that I certainly was. I was looking forward to his calls more than Joe's. He seemed to always be able to cheer me up or to keep me motivated and focused on my immediate concerns, which were to make the feds happy with tapes and to try to keep myself out of jail. He was a huge help to me and every day that passed, it seemed as though Joe and I were growing farther apart and Richie and I were growing closer. Any more, when warning bells started clanging in my head about the fact that this guy was a hardened criminal and what was I doing, what was I thinking? I turned that voice off and ignored my basic instincts, which up to that point had, for the most part, not failed me. I guess that I was beyond caring anymore. Richie was very convincing that he could definitely make sure that I never spent a day in jail. He told me that he would be out of jail in a month or so, and that he would be in the feds' custody, to keep him safe until he testified in this huge trial. Richie said that once he was out, we could arrange to see each other for a few hours at a time, and both of us were aware that we were dying to jump into bed together. I was so very lonely and he made me feel like I still had a future, one that might include him whisking me away. I was so anxious to stay out of prison that I was getting very stuck on the idea of Richie and me riding off into the sunset together, into the safety of the federal witness protection program. It's almost funny how someone who had been through as much as I had and had seen as much as I had could still be so unbelievably naive.

It seemed that no matter what I was doing, I was torn by conflicting emotions. At every angle, practically every aspect of my life at that time was filled with a desperate confusion and this weird love/hate relationship with right/wrong. Oh! I was so torn about everything I was doing. I did not want to talk to Richie after seeing Joe, but before I could stop myself, I was loving him too, even though it was entirely different and I was so in love with Joe!

Whoever wrote the line, "What a tangled web we weave, when first we practice to deceive," or whatever, sure as hell knew what they were talking about. Who I was deceiving was mainly myself. Yet I was also deceiving Joe, as to the extent of my feeling for Richie. Richie had just left the jail where Joe was and the feds had moved him to MCC in Manhattan. He was being prepped for trial there and in the first stages of entering the witness protection program. Richie bragged to me that he knew where some bodies were buried and that he had lots of aces up his sleeve that he would use later to help me out. He no longer included Joe in any of his plans. I told Richie that I was firm in my doing what I was doing for the feds would benefit both Joe and I. Because of the great work that I was doing for the feds, I was able to make arrangements to visit Joe in jail. I was very excited about the visit, but I was also a bit apprehensive because of the distance that had come between us since Richie came into my life. I know that it was Joe who had put him there and that this was all going according to plan, but I felt very guilty over my growing attachment to this man who was not Joe. No matter what I was feeling inside, Joe needed me and I would not let him down, at least not completely. I knew that he had to feel so very isolated and alone, it would be good for both of us to see a familiar and caring face for an hour or so. For me, it was going to be great to see him, no matter what. I knew how lonely and scared that I was at times, and I was not even in jail, at least not the traditional kind. I still loved him very much, despite all the confusion that Richie was causing for me internally. I drove out to see him at the Somerset County jail. I waited to see Joe in this room and after a few minutes there he was, dressed in one of those awful jail jumpsuits. My poor sweetheart. It still breaks my heart just reliving it now. He looked great to me, considering where he had been for the last couple of months and the love that I felt for him rushed into me so strongly that it took my breath away. I was weak with it. He looked at me and I knew that he was feeling the exact same way. We rushed at each other and hugged fiercely. His lips sought mine and we kissed, deeply, hungrily. It took a guard to finally pry us apart. We had to sit across from each other at a table and we were allowed to hold hands, so we remained touching each others' hands and arms for the duration of the visit. Kissing was only allowed at the beginning and at the end of the visit. I did not want to leave him, yet I was already looking forward to our passionate good-bye embrace. It was so good to see him! We talked a bit formally at first, but within minutes we were laughing and back to normal. How I longed to just rip off his clothes and make love to him! I knew from the look in his beautiful brown eyes and the way he was stroking my arms that he felt the same passions as I. We told each other how lonely we were for each other and how we thought we were faring in our different situations. I explained to him that even though I was not in jail, I was living in a similar situation, I was just free so that I could communicate with Billy, and now Randy. He was concerned as always about what I was doing, but like I told him, what choice did I have? I was doing it for as much his benefit as my own. I said that whatever good came of my cooperation with the feds, that he was going to benefit equally with me. He said that he would do anything to keep me out of jail. Joe said that it was terrible, but that this place that he was in was actually the best one in New Jersey. It was a new facility and he said that it was very hard for him mentally and that he was also having a difficult time because he was a vegetarian and all they usually gave him to eat was a disgusting baloney sandwich. He said other than Richie, whom he did not want to discuss, he had a cellmate who was a real cool guy and for that alone he felt very fortunate. They actually had fun once in a while and I was relieved to hear him talking like that. That was my Joe; optimistic in the face of anything. We talked a little about the deals that we were expecting to get, the actual charges that we would eventually be pleading guilty to. How much time in prison we expected to get, realistically accessing what we were looking at and what we were doing with our respective lawyers. I mentioned that I was hoping that my work for the feds would help me to convince them that they should make the state prosecutors back off, that this was a federal beef and they could let it drop. Joe said that he wished me luck with that, because he figured (rightly, as it turned out), that the state had their teeth into us and were not going to let go. It was great being able to talk with him, my best friend, about these problems that we were both going through, and that no one else could really understand. Our families were being fantastically supportive and loving to both of us, but there was just no way for them to really appreciate what we were going through. And why should they? It was us that had gotten ourselves into this mess anyway, but no one knew better than Joe what I was feeling. Much too soon for both of us, it was time for me to leave and we were once again about to be separated, this time for almost three years. I clung to him and tried not to cry, to be strong and face the music that we had written together. We kissed again for the last time, trying not to let the time together end, but once again, a guard (at least gently) broke us apart and told me that I would have to go, like right now. I watched them escort Joe to the door and then in an instant he was gone, swallowed up by the system that we had violated. I sort of staggered to the exit, gathered up my purse and got the hell out of there, so damn glad that I could get in my car and drive away, but feeling so terribly guilty that Joe could not.

Immediately after he was done testifying, the feds would send him to some place under a new name and take care of him for one year, then he would be on his own. Richie told me that when that happened he would arrange for us to get married and that since I would be his wife, I would basically be immune to prosecution and I would go into the witness protection program with him and not have to serve even one day in jail for my crimes. It certainly sounded too good to be true, and of course it was. I still spoke with Joe about once a week, but I was going with the guy that could help me now, and that guy was Richie. He was so certain about our future that I found myself believing him totally. I wanted to, so badly. Richie grilled me about my credit standing, and once he found out that I had great credit, he told me that I should start getting a bunch of cash advances, because I could now afford to ruin my credit, since once I was married to him and had a new identity thanks to the federal government, I would have a new name and be able to start from scratch. In this way he convinced me to get a bunch of new credit cards at almost every store that he could think of and open a charge account there. Richie said that once I had opened up an account at a certain store, I should buy a bunch of stuff and then go back to the store later and return all of the stuff for cash. He also said that another way to go would be to get a bunch of gift certificates at a certain store and then buy stuff with them. Then I should return the merchandise, also for cash. Richie also got out of me that I had an American Express gold card and this really got him going. He told me to start buying a bunch of gold with the card and then I could turn around and sell the gold for cash. In this way, I was paying the bills, as well as buying him lots of clothes and stuff that he wanted to have while he was still in jail. I was very reluctant to charge a ton of stuff like Richie was suggesting. I told him that I could get into even more trouble committing fraud since when I filled out the information on all of the new applications that he wanted me to get, I would have to lie and say that I was self-employed, etc. Once again, he assured me that it would not matter in the long run, since I would have a whole new identity once he was out and that none of this could come back to me anyway. I was so enthralled with him at this point that I went along with this plan of his.

I really felt bad knowing that I was killing my excellent credit standing, something that I had been kind of proud of. I was still talking with Billy about once a week and Randy every so often. Billy wanted me to come down to Mexico so that we could talk about our plans for the future. I had discussed this with the agents working the case and they told me that I could not go. Once I was off American soil, I was basically out of their care, since it was out of their jurisdiction and if something were to go wrong, they would be powerless to help me. They were very much afraid that Billy would kidnap me or even kill me if I went there. I did not believe this myself, but they told me that it really did not matter if Billy did just want to meet with me for business, they couldn't risk it. The feds told me that I should stall Billy somehow, by telling him that because I was a fugitive I was afraid to cross the border. When I spoke with Billy the next time and conveyed these things to him, he understood but was determined to get me down there. He said that since he had never met me before face to face, it was important to him that he really knew who he was dealing with and that it was necessary for us to go forward. Billy also told me that his partner had told him that it was imperative that they both meet with me to decide how we were going to proceed with getting the network going again. Billy would ask me specifics about what I had been doing for Rudy. Once he realized how much I had been involved and that I was the one who had been renting warehouses, safe-houses, storage units, tractor-trailers, not to mention taking care of all the bills and transporting very large sums of money, he was even more adamant that I come down to his place in Mexico — and right away.

Since I needed to discuss all of this with the feds, I told him that I would think some more about it and get back to him within a few days. Billy said sure, but that he would take care of me and that I should not be worried about anything. He said that we would be great business partners and he could not wait to get started. Billy could be very persuasive and charming when he wanted to be. He was also flirting with me just the tiniest bit, but I caught it at once and purred right back at him that I was in fact dying to meet him, and would love to have him take care of me. He said he could personally guarantee my safe passage in and out of Mexico. He bragged that he basically owned the town and the police and that he would send one of his people to get me safely across the border. Once I was at his home, he said that no one would dare hurt me in any way. I would be his guest. Billy then sweetened the pot by telling me that we could make millions of dollars together, plus, he said, wouldn't I love to see him and we could party with all of the excellent dope he had . . . It was starting to sound real good to me and I had to remind myself that I was setting him up and that if he knew that, he would have me killed — or even do it himself. I also had to get myself back into the right state of mind about who the hell's side that I was on. I could really lose my perspective talking to him for awhile.

Once again, confusion reigned supreme in my tired, twisted and torn psyche. I have to reiterate again that it was always Richie and not the feds who would put me back on track again — motivating me to feel the way that I should feel about all of this dreadful stuff I was doing and letting me know that he loved me and was totally behind me one hundred percent. I knew that the feds did not care about me; they wanted Billy so badly that they could taste him and every new tape that I gave them was getting them closer to capturing him. I was just a formality to them. They would still, of course, not hesitate to convict me of whatever they finally decided to pin on me, but they would be a hell of a lot more lenient than they would have been had I not been cooperating with them. I would have been rotting in jail, like Joe. They were seeing real results with me and at least treated me pretty decently for my efforts.

It was at this time that the agents in Phoenix really came into the picture. Once it was obvious that Billy really wanted to meet with me, they decided to get more involved in what we were going to do next. Obviously, Billy could not be put off forever. He would know that something was fishy and that would be that. I was informed that I needed to attend a meeting with a Phoenix customs agent and also a woman from the DEA in Arizona. They were flying in the next day to meet with me to discuss what our next move would be and how to proceed with Billy's demands that I go to him in Mexico. I arrived at the place where this meeting of the minds was to be held, introductions were made and we got down to business.

I was once again interviewed extensively about my involvement in this organization, and what I had been doing since my surrender at the end of June. I told them that Billy would never come back across the border. He had confided to me during one of our cozier conversations that he was a wanted man in the US and that there was no way that he was going to put himself in a position of getting busted on American soil. I said that for me to try to convince Billy otherwise would be a real bad move, as it would be an insult to him if I were to push a point that was so obviously not in his favor. They agreed with me and asked me what I thought could be done, since Billy would not come here and I could not go there. I told them that I really did not know what to do. If I continued to refuse to see him, everything would be over shortly, because to him and his mysterious partner, I could not work with them and the organization until we had all met and talked. One of the Arizona people, a guy who worked for the Customs Office, suggested that maybe I could be brought down to Tucson and convince Billy that since he could not cross the border and I was scared to do so, maybe a compromise could be worked out and I could meet with someone other than Billy himself in Arizona. This seemed like a fairly reasonable request for me to make to Billy, and after going over a few scenarios, they decided that perhaps I could convince Billy that I first needed to meet with someone like Gordo, his right-hand man in Arizona, with whom I was already familiar and vice versa. Maybe I could still hold onto my credibility with Billy and his people, without having to actually meet with him at all.

It was worth a try, so I told them that I would tell Billy that I was going to travel to Arizona and he could hook me up with Gordo once I got down there, and maybe we could all figure out a way for Billy and I to meet without compromising either one of our positions and freedom.

I drove back home to Princeton. I was nervous to have to talk to Billy that night. I mean, if I was on the run from the law and needed him to work and stay safe, why wouldn't I just do what he wanted and go to Mexico for the meeting? If this had really been happening the way that I had been telling Billy, I would not have hesitated to go and see him, so we could all start making money again. I needed them and they needed me. Since I was only pretending to be a fugitive, I would have to make believe that I was in fact scared to go into Mexico and make sure that I was able to convince Billy that I would eventually meet with him at his place once I was reassured by someone like Gordo. However, it was all I had and I would do my best.

Later that night, I put a fresh tape in the recorder and drove for about an hour or so to call Billy. We bullshitted for a few minutes and then of course he asked me when he was going to see me. I asked if maybe he could arrange for someone I knew, like Gordo, to meet with me first in Tucson and then we could go from there. Billy said it was a good idea and Gordo could personally take me into Mexico, since he went back and forth all the time. Billy then asked me how fast could I get to Arizona, as he was very anxious to get working again. Every day was costing him millions . . . Also, that he wanted very much to meet me, we would have a blast and get high together and who knew what else. I confess that I was attracted to this bad boy quite a bit and if it were not for the fact that I was working for the feds (and in love with Richie and Joe already; I must have an amazing amount of love to give), I would have went down there, partied and slept with him in a minute. I had grown quite fond of him and even though I knew what I was ultimately setting him up, it seemed easy for me to forget about that and imagine myself really doing this. I was screwed up? I was so beyond screwed up, I was ripped and torn up emotionally. I told Billy that I had a bit of work that I had to do before I left, but that I could be in Arizona within a few days. He said that was great and he was so looking forward to seeing me. We flirted a bit before hanging up and then I flicked the recorder off with another great tape to my credit.

I paged the agent before I left and he called me back right away. I told him that I had set everything up like we discussed and Billy was waiting for me to call him once I got to Tucson. I needed to be there in a couple of days, was that a problem? I went back home and got there in time for Richie's call that night. He was very excited for me and told me that this would be a real feather in my cap. I wanted to know what it was like to wear a wire, since the agents had told me that when I met with Gordo, I would have to tape our conversation and I would have to be set up with a body recorder, a device that could be concealed on my person. Richie assured me that it was no big deal and that I would do fine. I was a pro now, and he knew that I would be great. I really loved hearing this, from him especially, someone who had done all of this and more. Plus I was in love with him and his approval meant a great deal to me by this point. I heard from the FBI the next morning. I needed to meet them at their headquarters to get my plane tickets and instructions. The feds from Arizona had already left and would meet my flight in Phoenix. I had contacted my attorney about everything that was going on so that she would be aware of my movements. She was also sure that things would go fine for me as long as I did everything that the agents told me to.

That would prove way too hard for me.

She wished me luck and asked me to call her when I returned from Arizona. I packed a bag and went to the FBI for my instructions. The plane ride to Phoenix went smoothly and I have to admit that I was enjoying the free trip back to Arizona, which is a place that I love. Once I stepped off the plane, there were three agents waiting for me: the DEA agent and Customs guy I had met in New Jersey, but a new guy too. He was an Arizona FBI agent and was a very pleasant guy.

I did not realize at this time that all the stuff that I had been doing was more than a normal cooperating defendant does. I was in actuality assisting them in their efforts as opposed to merely talking a lot about people, places and things that I had either done or had some first-hand knowledge of. I was like an active participant in this investigation. I also was not really aware of the danger I was putting myself in. Foolishly, I still thought of this as kind of a difficult maze or a challenging game, and that I was not personally at risk. Richie had been more aware of this than I had, but I always brushed off his concern for my safety. He would get angry at me for doing all of these things for the feds without any real promises from them in writing, and he was constantly pushing me to make them put me in the witness protection program. Once we finally got into Tucson, we went to one of their offices for more interviews. It seemed that there was never enough that I could tell all of these people. I was continually answering the same questions over and over again. We also did some paperwork, and the customs agent, Steven, told me that he was what they called my contact agent and that while I was in Arizona with them, and even once I went home, he would be somewhat my boss as far as their investigation went. He was the one whom I was to contact in any event, and that was okay with me. I liked him.

I filled out some more paperwork at his behest and for the very first time since I had self-surrendered to the authorities, I was fingerprinted and they took a picture of me. They had a file that they kept of informants and now I was one of them. I have to say that this bothered me greatly. The next morning I woke up to the phone ringing. Steven was on the line and he asked me how soon I could get ready to see them. I asked him to give me an hour and I jumped in the shower. Then we sat around for awhile discussing various strategies for making this meeting between Gordo and myself happen. They explained to me how I would record my conversations with Gordo once I was with him. I would have a small recorder that I could keep buried in my purse, but was it sensitive enough to pick up everything that was said between us. By this time, several hours had passed and a few of us piled into a car and drove to the mall so I could attempt to contact Billy. When we got to the mall, we all went inside and I found a pay phone and paged Billy. I knew that he would immediately see from the number that I paged him with that I was in Arizona and I figured that he would call back fairly quickly. I was right. About five minutes after I paged him, my own beeper went off, and I told the agents that Billy was waiting for me to call him. They were all so excited that I felt like maybe none of them really believed that I had been talking with him for the past three or four weeks. Did they think I was making this up, or what?

They wanted me to page Gordo from a different location, so we drove to a pay phone outside of a convenience store off of the main highway. We all hung out for awhile, waiting for him to call me back. When he had not returned my page after about fifteen minutes, the agents were visibly deflating right before my eyes. I asked them if they wanted me to try again and they told me to wait a few more minutes. After another five minutes with no response from Gordo, I told them that maybe for some reason the page had not gone through, and that I wanted to try him again. This time, after about ten minutes, the phone rang and we all jumped. I called Billy back and he was glad to know that I was in Arizona. I let him know that I was holed up in a motel in Tucson, waiting for a meeting with Gordo whenever he wanted. I told him that I was reluctant but willing to make the trip into Mexico, but I also felt that I needed to kind of feel out the situation, hence the meeting with Gordo. I wanted to go forward with him and his partner, but I did not want to get arrested. Billy was understanding and said that he hoped that I would decide to come down and see him regardless. He told me that I should get together with Gordo and we would all take it from there. I was kind of shocked that he was being so nice and understanding about my feigned anxiety about a stupid trip into Mexico. He obviously wanted me to go there very badly, but he also did not want to let on how really important it was to him. All this time while I was talking with Billy, I had three agents huddling practically over my shoulder, listening intently to everything that I was saying. I told Billy that I would call Gordo as soon as I got off the phone with him. I also managed to have the presence of mind to mention that I was here now, but that I might have to leave suddenly if I got a call from some people I had been doing some work for in Philadelphia. I had thought to myself that I needed to leave myself an opening if I suddenly left the state, something that would not make Billy too suspicious. Since I had been telling him about these people from the start, I went ahead and told him that I really wanted to work for him, but right now they were paying me fairly decent money that I needed badly and I might have to split. I also secretly thought that Billy might still want me to work for him whether I met with him or not. But he could still call my bluff at any time, because I already knew something he did not: there was no way that I was going to Mexico to see him. I told him that I would rather work for him than these other people, but that I had to go where I could work and get paid. Billy again assured me about how much he wanted us to work together, that we could make millions of dollars and that he really hoped that I would decide to come to see him at his place in Mexico. Once I hung up with him, the agents were all real excited about the phone call and they immediately hustled me out of the mall and back into the car.

It was, of course, Gordo, and after a few minutes of greetings between us, we got down to business. I asked him if he had spoken to Billy about our getting together and he told me that he was aware of everything and that he would be willing to meet with me later that evening if that was okay for me. I answered that tonight was perfect. He told me to meet him at a sports bar in the middle of Tucson. The agents were all very excited again and we piled back into the car and drove back to the hotel so they could all get together and make plans for me and my night out. I guess that they assumed that I would only be with Gordo for around an hour or so, because they did not give me a second tape. Then they went over the rules with me. I was to meet Gordo at the place he specified, but under no circumstances was I to get into his car and leave. I would not see them, but the agents would be around at the sports bar, and it was important for my safety that I do everything that they were telling me now. I wanted to question the logic of this, but they shut me up and went on amongst themselves. I was a bit nervous to be doing this with Gordo, but I was also quite excited and eager to get going. As the appointed time drew near, they gave me the keys to my old Arizona car, and I took off after hearing their admonitions about straying from the bar with Gordo one more time. I myself was thinking that if he in fact did invite me to go off with him, I would probably ignore their orders and do it. What did they know about the world of drug trafficking? I would look real bad if I did not just hang out with him and he very well might be testing me to see what I would do. I would obviously have to play it by ear, but I told myself that I would follow my instincts and not necessarily their orders.

I found the place after cruising for a few minutes. It was a sports bar adjoined to a hotel and in the days when I had spent a lot of time in Tucson I had passed it often, though I had never been inside. The interior was a bit dark after the brightness of a Tucson sunset and I let my eyes adjust before looking around the bar for Gordo. I had clicked on the tape recorder before I walked in, so that it would not be a problem afterwards. I did not see him right off, so I sat down at a table and ordered a beer and waited. Gordo came up to my table after a couple of minutes and it appeared as though he had been lurking somewhere in the dark background, waiting for me to come in, probably to make sure that I was alone. Gordo greeted me very pleasantly and we just chatted for a minute; and then we started talking more seriously about all the bad stuff that gone down back in New Jersey and how everybody had been arrested, and what I had been doing since I had become a fugitive. I mentioned the people that I had been supposedly working for in Philadelphia and the fact that I was not crazy about them, but for now it was paying the bills and until Billy and I could resolve whatever, I was going to be going back fairly quickly. I explained to him, as I had to Billy, that I was uneasy about crossing the border with my fugitive status and also the fact that I might somehow get stuck down there.

At this point, I had ordered another beer and was beginning to feel a slight buzz. Gordo had also loosened up considerably and was leaning in to talk to me in a very confiding way. We started to talk about the cocaine bust that had gone down in Tucson right before the rest of the load had made it safely into California. He was telling me that those people were still in jail and that one of the guys had started talking to the feds but that the girl who had been arrested was holding up real well. Then he said that most chicks were tougher than guys and if he had to choose between a guy standing up or a girl, he would pick the woman every time. I was pleased to hear this and before long he was telling me a bunch of other stuff about Billy's operation down in Mexico and what had been going on down there for the last few months. I was now drinking like my third or fourth beer and was getting pretty buzzed. I was also having a blast and had begun to forget what had brought me there in the first place. I admit at this point that I was beginning (once again) to lose my perspective on the whole situation and had begun to think of myself as an outlaw again. I was truly enjoying Gordo's company and did not want our time together to end. I had to pee suddenly, and so I excused myself for a minute and went into the bathroom. At this point I remembered the tape recorder in my purse and I tried to turn it over. It was hard for me to do because I was kind of drunk and I somehow managed to get it together. I came back out to the table where Gordo was and he suggested that we go to another place that he knew of. I saw no reason not to go, despite what the agents had told me; and I knew that if I had turned him down, he would have been suspicious. I mean, where the hell else did I have to go? Any excuse that I even might have tried to run past him would have been incredibly lame. So in the interests of justice, I followed him outside and got into his car. I almost wish I could have seen the faces of those agents who were hanging out and watching over me. I bet they were out of their minds, when I drove off with Gordo. I was into this now and I was going all the way.

We only drove for a few minutes when he pulled into another parking lot. I guess the feds were afraid that he would kidnap me or something if I got in his car, but he just wanted to go to another place and drink some more. I also think that, to Gordo, this was a last bit of testing to make sure that I was not with the cops, or else I would not have left with him. That was where the agents I was working with were so wrong; I had to leave with him, since meeting with him and Billy was the only reason that I was supposedly in Tucson anyway. I decided then and there that I was going to draw this thing out for as long as I could. I was pretty blasted by now and enjoying myself immensely. Gordo was good company and it had been so long since I had gone out drinking and having fun. I actually thought to myself that I had gotten a lot of great stuff on tape and that the rest of the night was for me. Gordo brought up the work that I was doing in Philadelphia, and I explained to him that it was in the same line as what I had been doing for Rudy. I told him that I had not gotten paid for a while and that was one of the reasons that if these people contacted me in the next day or so, I would have to leave almost immediately. Gordo asked me if I needed any money and then handed over $200 and told me to take it and that he would not take no for an answer. I was touched by this gesture and so I pocketed the money and downed my drink and ordered another. We finished the next round and then he asked me if I wanted to go to another place that he knew of. The next place was a very small bar, very dark and Spanish. There was no way that the feds could have followed me into this place. It was way too intimate and I knew that, for as long as I was in there, I was actually alone with Gordo. He mentioned something to me about cocaine. I said, what did you say? He laughed and asked me if I still did coke. I said sure, and so then he handed me a bindle and told me that I should hit the bathroom and try some out. Of course I did, as I was very high by now. I snorted some and it was really good stuff. I went back out to the bar area and sat back down. Gordo said that Billy had just paged him and he was going to call him back. He got up to make the call and I put some of the coke on my fingernail and snorted it sitting at the bar. I had not a care in the world! I was completely crazy, all right. When he came back I was flying now and I told him that I was ready to drive to Mexico right now, let's get in the car and go. I was serious too. He kind of laughed and said that he was too drunk to go now; we could go in the morning. I was like, come on! I'm ready to go right now! I stashed the rest of the coke in my wallet and we left to go to another place. I'm thinking that the agents must be pretty pissed at me right now, but I am putting on a very convincing act for Gordo and that they should be happy about it. Obviously, he was not looking to kidnap me or he would have done it by that point. They probably should have let me go into Mexico. I bet everything would have been cool and I would have actually gotten a ton more information about Billy. Because when I think about it, if Billy had intended to harm me from the first as the agents feared, all Gordo would have had to do was let me get drunk while he stayed relatively sober. Once he had got me into the car even once, driving me across the border and away from any possible help, and once I was in Billy's domain, that was it. The last place that we went was a more public watering hole and we sat at the bar for a couple of hours talking about business and more of what had been happening since Rudy got arrested and the whole New Jersey end had gone down in flames. It was obvious to me, even as high as I was still, that Gordo was trusting me completely at this point. I knew that no matter what happened and whatever lame reason I wound up giving Billy for not going down to Mexico, I would still be okay with them. Finally, Gordo asked me if I wanted to call it a night and he said that he would drive me back to the sports bar where my car was still parked. Gordo dropped me off at my car and we said goodnight. I got in and he watched me drive away. I did not even look for the feds that I knew still had to be around. I drove straight to the hotel where I was staying, and once I had parked the car, I was instantly surrounded by federal agents. I was still a bit drunk, but much more sober than I had been a couple of hours before. I also had decided that I would hand over the money that Gordo had given me, but that I would tell them nothing about the cocaine that he had given me, and which I still had quite a bit of. I wanted to keep that for myself. The agents hustled me inside quickly and snatched the car keys from me. Once we got inside the room where the rest of them were waiting for me, they asked me for the tape and I took the tiny recorder out of my purse and handed it over to them. They started in on me about leaving with Gordo, but as I've already mentioned my reasons for doing as I did, it suffices to say that I went into the same type of explanation for them, adding that doing things my way had greatly added to my credibility with Gordo, and of course through Gordo, to Billy. They agreed, but were still all frazzled from my cowboy antics. They all listened to the tape that I had made of the early evening conversations and then grilled me for hours about what had been said after the tape went off. I told them everything I could remember about what we had spoken about and when I got around to the part where Gordo had given me some money, I reached into my purse again and handed Steven (the customs agent) the 200 bucks that Gordo had given me.

They told me that they had been freaking out from the moment that I had gotten into Gordo's car and driven off. A few of them had wanted to blow my cover and get me out, but at least a few of them had believed in what I was doing and let me continue. I told them that I was sorry to have worried them, but that once I had gotten going, I could not stop with Gordo and it had worked beautifully. Gordo had told me all sorts of things that I could never have known from some telephone calls. I told them that they should feel like I did about the whole thing; that it was a terrific success and I felt now that whether I went to Mexico or not, Billy was still going to be talking to me and attempting to set up our network again. I told them that I had set it up with Gordo that I could be disappearing at any time, and I thought because of the night that I had spent hanging and drinking with him, that my credibility was so high that my appearance was not going to be the issue anymore. It turned out that I was right.

The agents were quite happy with the tape and the additional information that I imparted to them afterwards. For reasons that were never altogether clear to me, they packed me up and got me the hell out of town the next morning. I asked them about what I should tell Gordo or Billy when they tried to contact me? I mean, I knew what I would say, but I wanted to hear it from them. They just told me to stick with the story about the people that I was supposedly working for in Philadelphia, that they had called and required my presence immediately. Secretly, I thought that the feds figured me to be unpredictable as far as they were concerned. I still think that they thought I might have snuck off to Mexico behind their back somehow. So they got rid of me. Probably the right move, because I just might have gone to Mexico . . . somehow. I was a wild card. Once I got back to New Jersey, I of course heard from Billy almost immediately. He's like, what the hell happened to you? Last that I heard you had this great night with Gordo and then the next day you were gone. All I could tell him was that the guys that I was working with on the East Coast had called me up later that night after I had left Gordo and demanded my immediate return. What could I do? They owed me money, I told him, and they wanted me to rent them a place right away. I told Billy that I was really sorry and that if he could not continue trying to work all of this out with me anymore, I understood his position completely. Billy responded like I thought he might; that he no longer deemed it necessary for me to come to him in Mexico, that we would continue to talk and to make something happen very soon. I would be working directly with Randy on the project, and as soon as possible Randy would be flying out to see me in New Jersey. I told Billy that that sounded great. Billy told me to stay in touch with him as much as possible, but that he also wanted me to talk to Randy much more in the coming weeks. He gave me a pager number for Randy and told me that I should try to call him the next day and set something up for the next week or so. I told Billy that it would be my pleasure and on that note I hung up and shut off the tape recorder. I called up the FBI agent in Jersey and told him about what had gone down in Tucson and then about the phone call that I had just taped with Billy. He was thrilled with the news that we were still going forward with everything, and with the additional exciting possibility of nailing Randy right here in New Jersey.

They released Richie only a couple of days later. He called me from a safe-house that the feds had stashed him at. Richie said that there was guys with him 24 hours a day, but that it was just fantastic to be out of jail. He also mentioned that one of his first requests as a free guy, not to mention federal star witness, was to see me right away. He told me that it would be kind of a big production for the feds to let me meet with him, but that as long as they were sure that I wasn't being followed to the meeting site, we were in business. The feds would bring him to some undisclosed place and I would drive over and meet them in my car. At that point, I would follow the car with the feds and Richie in it and we would drive to a hotel that they had already picked out. I was going to have to drive way down south for these little get-togethers, but in actuality, I had no problem with that since I was finally going to get together with this man that I had changed part of my life for. We set up to meet at a certain parking lot area off the Garden State Parkway the next day at around two in the afternoon. We were both pretty excited about finally being able to get together after all of these months, and finally jump into bed, like we had promised each other.

I was kind of nervous about finally meeting him, though. It was finally sinking in that I really did not know him except for hundreds of very personal and exciting phone conversations, but what the hell? I was not going to back out of anything at this point. I arrived at the parking area as I had been instructed. I was looking all around, all the way there, in case someone had been following me. Finally this car pulled up alongside where I was parked and I saw Richie sitting in the back grinning at me. I grinned back and could not wait to be alone with him. He looked just great and all I wanted to do was to be with him. One of the agents got out of the car and walked over to me. He introduced himself and so did I. He told me that I should follow them to a hotel that was about ten miles further south. I got back into my car and followed them to a decent hotel. I got out of the car and

Richie emerged from the fed vehicle. He looked great. We walked into the hotel together, him grinning at me continuously. I paid $100 for a room that we would be using for only two hours, which was all the time together that we were being allowed. I did not care, I just wanted to finally be with him in the same room, alone. I got the key and we walked hand in hand. I let us in and we closed the door behind us.

At some point, I heard from an agent who told me that they had arrested Randy for something or other, and it was all over. I was done. I felt horrible about Randy and I had an empty, strange detachment from my own feelings of betrayal and guilt and shame for what I had done. I was loathing myself inside and it would come out in a lot of different ways until I worked it all out within myself. It was weird to not have to go out and make calls, talk to agents . . . I was deflated and, as I had thought, once I was done, they were all just gone from my life with no promises or guarantees of any kind for what would become of me. I saw Richie just two more times before he was also seemingly out of my life and I was back on my own. Richie   asked me what I thought of him and I told him that he was great and when could I kiss him? He told me to go right ahead and so I did of course. It was great, and what I had been waiting for. I held him tight and brought out a bottle of champagne and some cigars that I had brought for him. I also had a bag packed with all the clothes and things that I had been accumulating for him over the past few months. He told me between kisses how much he loved me and that this was the best day of his life. I breathlessly agreed with him and we fell down on the bed together. He was a fabulous kisser and I was being swept away by that alone. We made love with the passion stoked by months of frustration, and then we talked quietly while I got the champagne out of the ice bucket and ran the bath for a soak together. He was telling me about the case that he was going to be testifying for and what was going to happen afterwards. Richie once again mentioned that he wanted to marry me as soon as possible, he loved me and wanted me to go into the witness protection program with him. He also said again that with all of my cooperation and the couple of aces that he claimed that he still had up his sleeve, I would never see a prison cell. He knew that these were things that I wanted to hear and more, I wanted desperately to believe him and make these things a reality. I was still obviously terrified about the possibility of going to prison and I would have done almost anything to avoid it. We filled up a couple of glasses with the chilled champagne and climbed into the bathtub and held each other, kissing again. All too soon, it was time for us to have to leave. We kissed again for the last time that day and he gathered up all the stuff that I had brought for him, and then the agents were knocking on the door. I told him I loved him one more time, kissing him all over his face and neck, and let him walk out the door. I watched out the window as the agents hustled him back into their car and whisked him away from me. Later that night Richie called me from his secret hideout, and told me that he had loved being with me, and that he wanted to marry me and spend the rest of his life with me. I had to move into a new place and think about finding some kind of job in between all the other stuff I had going on.

I found a job soon after I moved and settled into a regular kind of life, even though I was still only awaiting my fate. I think it was July or August of 1995 that I last saw Richie. I was spending almost all of my time alone, and waiting for paperwork from the federal court or the state court. I was waiting for the date of my sentencing. I was getting really antsy waiting, and waiting. I had sporadic dealings with my family members by telephone. I would talk to Richie by phone as well; we still were talking about the feds finally doing something with my paperwork and sticking me in the program with him. There were days when I would actually get excited and hopeful of it happening, after all.

Finally I got some mail from the Federal Court or the US Attorney's office and learned that I had a sentencing date. It was in mid-September, 1995 — just about two weeks away from when I received the letter. I remember vaguely talking with Richie about the sentencing; he was thinking that I could easily just get straight probation — look at all the stuff I had done for them. I did possess a very wonderfully supportive letter from the US Attorney's office in Arizona, whom I had really made happy with my efforts "undercover." It was a glowing letter; I still have it and I am grateful to them to this day for their kindness and (for the most part) understanding. I thought the letter sounded like it would woo any judge to go easy on me; I had really done a tremendous amount. Randy was locked up, and it looked like he might go to trial. They would want me to testify. I was not looking forward to anything like that ever really happening. It was one thing to just do things on telephones and even the one time with Gordo . . . but to have to sit there and talk about all of this in court in front of them, well, that was something I could not even contemplate. I had a lot of problems with what some call "flipping"; I wasn't really ashamed of what I had been doing but I was not altogether proud of it either. It all just felt — slimy. Sometimes you just do the best you can and whatever happens, you just deal with it. It was like thinking about the fact that at that time, Billy was still out there in Mexico. Did he know my real name? Was he actively looking for me? What did he know? My pager had been taken by agents in New Jersey shortly after I got back from Phoenix. I guess I am simply trying to make you partially understand what the waiting time for everything in between everything else felt like to me. Sometimes it was just unreal; Salvador Dali paintings have always fascinated me and it felt like I was living in one, sometimes.

But I remained upbeat in my own inimitable fashion. I listened to what everyone in my life had to say about what they thought would happen. I longed to get all of this over with. I had to finally know my Fate, as it was certainly not in my hands any longer. I had done everything I could for them and so I waited the day out, sweating a little while I tried to just work and pretend everything in my life was normal like everyone else's. I took the day of the sentencing off work; no matter what the judge's decision was, I wasn't just going back to work. Whatever it would be, I needed to deal with it alone as much as possible. I could just see getting like eight years or something terrible and trying to function at work. If they just cart me off to jail, well, that would solve that dilemna.

Ben, my supportive boss and good friend, was so cool about everything at the end. I was a real basket case actually. I would be such a bitch and I was weepy and just really on edge and probably miserable to be around for months. The uncertainty of my future and the limbo of my present were taking their toll after almost 18 months of living like this. Seemed like a million years. I met my federal attorney, Tonianne, at her downtown Newark, New Jersey office, and together we walked and talked our way over to the Federal Building, right around the corner and up a few blocks. I was very nervous. Just very uncomfortable, in a nice dress and heels, and wondering what this was going to be like and would I be going home this very afternoon? Would I be locked up? I was very nervous, but curious enough to keep walking forward. We got inside and sat down.

Oh no! There was Stretch! Yes, our old friend Stretch was also being sentenced today. I did not hear what kind of sentence he received, however, and I did not even want him to see me, so I kind of huddled down and watched him walk out of the courtroom. Damn, why couldn't Joe be here today, too? They called us next and I walked up to the plate. My lawyer presented all the wonderful things I had done for the feds since I surrendered and she also had several commendation letters from the law enforcement agencies, stating that my work for them was to be acknowledged and they all recommended leniency against me. The judge had all this stuff to look at and even the US attorney was talking like I had really gone the extra mile. The judge starts talking about this and that and I was on pins and needles. Just say it! He is blabbing about considering this and that, but I certainly was a key player, an integral part of this organization, and "you shall go to prison (or words to that effect) for 42 months. . ." 42 MONTHS? Oh . . . I felt crushed, devastated, and while I realize that I was looking at doing 87 months (that was the original sentence from the US attorney), and this was more than half cut, I admit to feeling very upset that after everything that I had done I was still going to be spending three and a half years of my life in prison.

I could barely stand there. I wanted to cry and scream and run away. I stood there stoically and none of this showed on my face. He was now talking about the fact that I had done all this and I obviously was not a flight risk and that I would be allowed to leave and I would surrender to the prison facility on a yet-to-be-determined date. This was a huge relief and I forgot for a moment about the prison thing and felt so grateful that I would be going home tonight. Thank you, Goddess. Then Tonianne was asking the judge about that I was requesting to leave New Jersey during the time that I was waiting for the Bureau of Prisons to tell me where to go. She explained to the judge that I wanted to be with my family members before I went to prison, after all this time in New Jersey alone. He was kind-hearted enough to grant this request. This was great news too. I could go to some semblance of normalcy before heading out to the Big House. I had already spoken to my sister about this being a possibility and she was all for it, which was wonderful. There was some more talk and signing of papers and such, I really don't remember clearly. I walked out in a semi-daze, both elated and devastated. Very weird state of mind. I hugged Tonianne and thanked her for everything she had done for me. I would see her again, years later, and she would help me again.

I went home and felt numb. I had to arrange to leave. I had to tell Ben, my boss, that I was definitely going away. I had to talk to Richie. I had to lay down and curl up in a ball and cry inconsolably for awhile. So many things to do. It's hard to describe; I just kind of did everything in a semi-trance state. I just really wanted to wake up from this insane dream that I was having and be back to my "real" life. I had to wrestle with myself because this was my real life and I needed to get a grip.

My boss took the news well. He said that I always had a job with him and would I please keep in touch? Once I got out of New Jersey and to my sister's house in southern California, I tried hard to relax for however long I was being allowed to be "free." I was so grateful to be out of New Jersey and with someone in my family, someone who loved me, that I could talk to — until I was told where to report to prison. The waiting was agonizing; at this point, knowing that I was definitely going to prison for 42 months, which seemed like an eternity after all the stuff I had already done. I had to grieve for myself and what had happened. I then worked on accepting what was to be, which I accomplished through smoking a lot of very good weed and bonding deeply with a kitten that my sister had lovingly bought for me.

I would call this phone number of the Bureau of Prisons and I would attempt to find out if they had processed my paperwork yet. Where would I be going? When would I have to report? All of these questions, with their tag-along uncertainties and fear, plagued me when I allowed them too. I smoked more pot and tried not to dwell on what I did not know, what I could not control, and to not let myself assume how it would be to go to prison. I was terrified. I had tried so hard to avoid this, and despite all the efforts I had put forward, one man, a judge, had just condemned me to go to jail for almost 4 years. Ah . . . I cried self-pitying tears and sobs of anger and fright, defiance and sorrow for all that could have been, for not only me, but Joe and Randy. . .

I was so without any spiritual guidance at this point. Totally bereft of any meaning in my life. Its a small miracle that I did not just run away or do away with myself. It is surprising to me now the depth of my strength, even then. I wound up just chilling at my sister's house for almost three long months before I got word that I had to report to the Federal Prison Work Camp in Phoenix, Arizona on December 18th, 1997. I had to buy my own ticket to surrender myself to prison! That was a tough one. It was a minimum security facility; no cells, no locks, no guns, no razor wire. That was a relief to me. At least I did not have to go into what I still think of as a "real" prison, the kind in the movies that I dreaded having to deal with. Looking at it from a different angle, however, perhaps after all I had done for law enforcement, cooperating and virtually acting as an undercover agent, risking my life, it would not have been unjust for me to have received straight probation, or a house-arrest type of scenario. But I had been sentenced to go to prison, and to prison I would go. I bought my first one-way airline ticket, ever, and attempted to mentally ready and prepare myself for what was to come. But what loomed before me especially in my mind, was that I did not know what this would be like. I had nothing to really prepare me to be confined for any length of time, much less 42 long months.

I was still in touch with Richie and he was doing pretty well adapting to the new environment that the feds had put him in. He was still telling me that he was trying to get the feds to do the paperwork that would get me into the program with him. I just could not even hold onto that as any hope anymore and I argued with him to face reality (as I was really trying hard to do myself) and listen! I was going to prison. For awhile. This was in motion and it wasn't going to stop. I needed him to support what was going to happen and be there for me and love and reassure me that I would be okay and not to keep talking about something that was basically just a fantasy anymore in my mind. I had to get used to this fact of prison. He would stubbornly stick to his script that he was still working on it and it would happen. I loved him for saying this and I also hated him for it. More torn and conflicted feelings going on. I started to talk to him a little less and just played with my kitten and smoked my sister's weed. I was pretty content for the most part; just sick of waiting. Word finally came in the form of a letter that told me when and where to report. At last. A date. Coming up in about one month from now. I am — will be — going into prison.

More numb and unbelieving emotions to deal with that I more or less drowned out in pot. But any true bud smoker knows that pot can also accentuate the stuff you are already feeling and in my own convoluted way, I was dealing with this and I would be there as directed. I was ready to get this over with after so much waiting around for its inevitable occurrence. I had a little money, because I managed to buy the ticket to Phoenix. I would have to take a cab to the prison from the airport. I was having definite issues about this total loss of freedom. I had found out that this place was minimum security but I really did not know what that meant. It was prison, no? I worried a lot about what this was going to be like and how would I adapt to this total change in lifestyle. I couldn't leave! No matter how badly I wanted to! I was really wrestling with myself as to how much I could take. Then I would think of my poor Joe. He had to take way more than I had been handed, and I would try to let him inspire me to do the right thing and deal with the consequences of my actions and do so with dignity and strength and power.

I vowed to myself, and to the beautiful goddess who watched over me, that I would use this time away to really get into me. Who am I? What do I believe in? What is the purpose of my Life? What did I want to accomplish? Why had this happened? What was I thinking? I had to believe in my heart that not a moment of my life could be thrown into a trash can that said "waste." Life is too precious to ever want to look back and say, that time was wasted. I also felt empowered that this was in fact in my control and I could get through this ordeal any way that I chose to do so. I had been given this opportunity to reflect and be with my sister, and I was so lucky for those things, for the time. So I enjoyed it as well as I could.

The day finally came to leave. Vicki, my sister, drove me to the airport for the short flight from Ontario, CA to Phoenix. It was tearful and I just wanted her to leave because this was upsetting and I had to get a grip on what I was doing on this long-dreaded day. I think being an intuitive Pisces, she understood this and she did leave me to myself after big hugs and "be carefuls." I waited in line to board the plane, as I had done so many times before, but never like this. I had barely anything with me. I had called the prison to see what I was supposed to bring or what not, and it was like — bring nothing. Clothes on my back. Period. Once I got in there, I could get some things sent in to me.

I was entering a totally alien world where I would be part of the community of felons. Would I be accepted and find friends? Would people there find out that I was a rat? Or would they already know? So many uncertainties. I was really scared. I did not even like being with other women all that much, I mean, as friends, even. I had not had a close female friend in a long time. I was going to be with them morning, noon and night. Oh, there was so much to play with in my mind! It never stopped so I stepped onto the plane so I could get answers to all this and quit driving myself crazy. Short hop to Phoenix; we were there in no time at all. I got right off and got a cab. I saw no point in waiting any longer. The man driving the taxi was very nice, a beautiful soul and very sorry to hear where I asked him to take me. I spilled my guts to him and he was so compassionate. What a blessing it was to talk with him before I got there! He was goddess-sent and I was actually relaxed and okay when we pulled up to the front of the place.

Prison. Here I am. Surreal, disbelief. Wake up! Bad dream! I paid him and tipped him as well as I could afford. I had some money that my mom had sent and my sister had given me. You had to pay for lots of things here, I was told. All I had were the clothes I was wearing, my glasses case with my glasses inside, a bottle of saline and my contact lens case, a pack of cigarettes and a lighter. I walk inside the building, holding my breath and just feeling like . . . oh it's so hard to describe this feeling! I had to muster up every ounce of courage I had to go inside, because I knew once I was inside, I was not coming out for a long time. It was a week before Christmas and I was going to be here for New Years and for my birthday and then for Thanksgiving. All at once, everything hit me and it was like being slugged, hard, in the stomach and having the wind totally knocked out of you. WHAM! I staggered for the door and they probably thought I was drunk. I was stoned, though. I had smoked with my sister before getting on the plane and I was still buzzed. It was not helping my feelings, it was only intensifying them. It was also killing that total warrior part of my soul to be submitting to this authority like a whipped dog. It made me sick that I was just going to hand myself over to them and not resist this loss of control, this loss of freedom, this obedience that they would demand, the humiliation of being ordered around and called by a number, not a person anymore. This was the culmination of everything I had fought against and it is the balance and sometimes irony in Life that had brought me here to experience this. I had to understand that there was a reason for this and I had to find it and understand it and learn and grow from it.

Could I do that inside a prison camp? I walked to the desk and announced myself. 42 months and counting down. The office was nice enough; from what I had seen, the place was recently built and still in good shape. I looked all around and out the doors and saw some girls walking around and staring in at me. I hate being the new girl anywhere. I felt like I was walking on very thin ice though and was so unsure of what to expect and how to proceed. Very timid feeling of powerlessness, one that I had barely ever experienced before. Never on this level. It was difficult to speak. My throat felt all closed up. Yet I found it within me to face this with strength and power. Barely.

I am feeling so utterly powerless that it is all I can do to not just burst into tears and just lay down and sob my heart out. Ghastly feeling, to be powerless. Stripped of your own choices. I was not doing very well, at this point. They take my money and tell me that they will apply this to my account and over the next several days they will make sure I see a doctor and I will be assigned a counselor and a case worker. They instructed me that I needed to memorize my number, they would call me with it over the loud-speaker and I better know that it was me they wanted. Oh, I just wanted to die. I asked how I was going to get more clothes to wear, ummm, like, this is all I have to wear until whenever? I was coldly informed that they would probably issue me the uniforms to wear for work on Monday. Monday? I am just going to hang out in these same clothes all weekend? That was indeed the case. I felt like just dying. This was just the most pathetic feeling. I couldn't fight them. I just stood there like a zombie and waited for whatever was next. One of the guards walked me out of the office and outside where we crossed the quad area and entered one of the buildings; I could see there were three larger ones as well. These were where we all lived. We neared the building she was taking me to and there were six or seven women hanging out on benches in the front, smoking. They were all staring at me and I felt like I was in a fishbowl, being scrutinized and appraised and sized up. I felt horribly self conscious and I looked at them and tried to smile; most of them smiled nicely at me, and I knew they remembered what it was like to come here. A few of them called out greetings and their names; I said hello and that my name was Linda. The guards in the office had given me a big roll of stuff, like a blanket and what not; and I hugged it to me and again just wanted to cry. I had been holding in tears for awhile now. I would not cry in front of any of these people. I had to be strong. I kept having to dig deeper into my Self to find the strength and composure that I needed. I kind of waved at them, and followed the guard into the building where I saw my new home for the first time. It was actually pretty nice inside, but there were no actual rooms; it was like cubicles, almost, and it appeared that in this tiny space, two women lived together. There were no doors or anything. Just open cubicles. There was recessed lighting all up and down the place, it was never dark in there, always light, which is good and bad depending on the perspective you choose. She walked me down to one of the cubicles on the end and there was a woman sleeping on the bottom bunk. Of course, we had bunk beds. My new roommate. She groggily sat up and introduced herself. Her name was Terri. She apologized for being sick and she seemed very sweet despite the fact that she was all sick and I was just like in a dream, thinking that none of this is real, when would the joke be over? I was left there by the guard, who told me that I could do whatever I wanted until someone called me to their office or to a guard station. They escorted me out of the office itself and outside, walking toward these cemented walkways where I could now see the inside of the prison itself. It was like a large quad; looked like a small college campus. Very tasteful and total desert, a southwestern look and feel, and everything was maintained beautifully and I could see why: women were wearing these awful green pants and yellow shirts and working here and there and taking care of everything. Oh boy. I was screaming inside to get out, leave, run, anything. I walked instead down the walkway and into a room that said something like, receiving, or check in, who knows. There I was told to strip and they did a total search of my person. Totally humiliating and it just gets you emotionally right where they want you. It was as close as I ever got to breaking, besides maybe one other time that we will get to later. There were two women guards in this room with me, big women that were performing this violation upon me. Right away they try to make you feel like you are nothing. They don't care about you one bit. Its such a weird energy; such detachment on their part except to bark orders at you and degrade you in some fashion, letting you know that they are in charge and they can do whatever they want to you. You have essentially lost all of your rights, not only as a citizen of the United States, but as a human being with certain rights to privacy and dignity and respect. Those are all gone. They want you to feel broken, so for a person like me, it was my duty to make sure that never happened. No one or no system would break me or my Spirit. The defiance in my heart has always worked for me and it did again at this very low point. Once they were done checking my body for drugs or weapons or whatever people tried to sneak in, I was told I could put my clothes back on again. This was on a Friday. Most new inmates come in on Fridays. I then had to fill out a bunch of paperwork and they coldly informed me that I would have to send back my contacts and the saline solution; since they did not sell the solution here at the prison, I was not allowed to have contacts. Of course, they could not have told me this on the phone when I called. I could keep my glasses. Gee, thanks. I appreciate that you are allowing me to see. They also took my cigarettes and my light. You can't have a lighter here, they said. You can buy matches on commissary. I was addicted enough to my cigarettes that I protested and asked them if I could smoke at all here. They told me that lots of people smoked, of course I could smoke, but I had to buy my own from the commissary and I could not do that until it was open, in four days. Four days!? I ask them what I am supposed to do until then. Oh, "just make friends fast" or some sarcastic quip.

I had to learn where all those places were, because they sure didn't like it when they called you and you did not show up. You could get sent away to a medium security prison for that kind of stuff.

I put down the bedroll thing and thought that I should just go back outside (?) and not disturb Terri. She was out of it and I figured I would make up the paper-thin mattress later on. I really needed a cigarette and I would have to go and make friends. It was very hard to walk back out, though; felt like I was in mud, very thick and going forward was difficult, cumbersome. From where could I summon up the will to put on a decent face and have to communicate with these women? This was where I was living now. These women were my new community members. Small community, closed off totally from the world outside.

Weird vibe once I push myself out the door. I sit down on one of the benches and a black woman tells me her name and asks me if I want a smoke. I say yes, thank you, my name is Linda; they took my cigarettes and my lighter! This breaks the ice, because she knows; they did it to her too. She is fairly pleasant but I am so wary of all of them and feel like a kitten among older, wiser alley cats. That sounds stupid, based on everything else I have related, but I was so unsure of how to act and if anyone was going to be openly hostile and what would I do? Very wary. I was talking to a few others as well; they were actually all very nice and I was starting to relax just a little. It was just so weird to be sitting here like this and I am thinking that this is to be my existence for 42 months. I had to fight back the closing-throat feeling; is that panic? It's always been more difficult for me to make friends with women, and it crossed my mind that I was being forced to deal with that issue and I needed to try to embrace the good that I could find. Sounded good, in my head, but I could not do that yet.

I forget a lot of the early stuff there; I was really numb and detached and freaking out inside and trying to be composed and act like nothing was going on. The one black woman who had given me the smokes went inside her building and brought out a pack for me and gave me some matches too. She said I could pay her back whenever I could. If I needed some more, I could come to her. You see these stupid prison movies and I wondered if I would like owe her something and was I her bitch now? Stupid stuff, but these kinds of thoughts were racing in my tired, miserable mind. It certainly did not seem like any movie I had ever seen. It was pretty mellow, actually, and I knew that I was so lucky to be here in this place with no cells and bars and razor wire. The place was pretty big. I walked around a little by myself, just trying to see where things were; we were out in the middle of the desert, near nothing except the men's medium security prison that was right down the road. The women told me that working certain jobs there, you could see the guys. I didn't really care but did not want at all to act like I was not into that, so I asked more questions and tried to act interested in everything. I was thinking about how I would have to go to the bathroom, and take a shower, eventually, and what would that be like? Every simple, ordinary thing that one normally takes for granted, like having privacy when you take a shower or going to the bathroom, is altered and you must adapt immediately to these changes, trying not to show too much emotion around anyone, not wanting to be seen as vulnerable. I was always a very modest bathroom type of person. I did not even like to go to the bathroom at work when I could help it. This was just being thrown into it and you had no choice but to sink or swim. Not in the actual survival sense, but mentally you had to set up a shield against whatever might possibly blow you off course as you aim to keep it together and let the days go by, one by one. I had been smoking lots of pot in the last three months, too, and there was going to be no more of that, so I was going to be jonesing a little for the next two or three days. Also not helpful.

I was also trying to get used to the way people talked and acted. It was different than on the "outside," and some of these women were very tough-looking, tough-talking and I was trying to learn who was cool and who was to be avoided. There was also an awful lot (I thought) of older women knitting and what not. I thought, what the hell could these old women have done that some cold-hearted judge is going to send them away from their families and grandchildren to go to prison? What are they supposed to be getting out of this? I felt sorrow and compassion for them and wondered how they coped. They actually looked fairly serene and I wanted to feel that way too. Maybe I could, in time. Because the prison itself was so like a college campus, it made the whole surreality of this experience complete. It was so open and you could almost image that you were away at school and not here, that you could leave if you wished. It did not seem like a prison and it encouraged me to entertain notions that it was not; that it was a weird dream that I was having. Prison is dark and cold and steel-clanging and bleak. This was light and open and airy and in some ways beautiful. That almost made it harder to come to accept that I was in prison that first day. It was almost like I needed it to be worse to accept what was happening. Then again, just all these people around was so different than any existence I had lived and everyone that saw me knew I was new and stared and would either be friendly, neutral, or semi-hostile. You could feel some of these women from across the way. Their energy was very aggressive and I did not want any part of that. I eventually went back to my room in the building and talked to Terri for awhile. I was insanely relieved to find her so very cool and nice and I was again being assisted in ways much higher than myself. Another woman came into see Terri and we exchanged greetings. This was Penny; Terri and she were lovers and had been before they were both sent to prison for running/knowing of a meth lab in Oregon, where they were from. They were both totally nice and did wonders to put me more at ease. I had friends, I thought. Thank you.

Terri made bead necklaces and wanted to give me one for Christmas. Everyone there was pretty subdued around the holidays, especially those who would have no visitors over the weekend or the holiday itself. That's what part of the energy I had been feeling was: depression and a low key sorrow that just pervaded the atmosphere. It was something else not to give in to. Almost immediately, Terri and Penny were talking to me about religion. They had been meeting with Jehovah's Witnesses even before they left Oregon and they were going to meetings here, too. Once a week, a couple would come in and they would study the Bible and have fellowship, etc. They wanted to know if I would be interested in coming with them. I was not at all sure that I would be into that, but they were my new friends and I wanted to feel close to someone here and I just said that would be cool, let me know when to go. I figured it would be something to do and people from the outside world to talk to. I liked to learn anyway, and it would perhaps be interesting to study the Bible while I was here. I would find lots of people who would come to that conclusion while they were in prison. You really needed something to hold onto, to find faith and hope in. I definitely was spiritually starved and required nourishment to make it through the next three and a half years. Sometime during that first day I went to eat with the other women at the appointed time. You had to stand in a long line and eat whatever they served. The women worked in the kitchen cooking, cleaning, and serving. I sure as hell did not want to work in the kitchen, and I had been told that most new girls were put into the kitchen to work. I had to find something else first, before they just assigned something to me.

I also met Terri and Penny's friend, Michelle. She was in for bank robbery. She was also very nice and these three women were to be my friends throughout my stay in Phoenix. Later on, when Terri was sleeping again and Penny and Michelle, who lived in a different building, had left, I made up my pitiful new bed. I had never seen such a thin mattress in my life. Wow. I quietly did these things as I listened to the sounds around me, which echoed in the open atmosphere of the place. I met most of my neighbors and almost everyone was really pretty nice and I was comforted by this fact. I lay down on my bed and just stared silently at the wall, hugging myself and trying not to cry. What a forlorn feeling it was to be surrounded by people going about their daily routines: women coming back to their cubicle (pods, they were called) and getting out of their uniforms, taking showers, noisy and yelling and laughter. Strange to hear all this and wondering how one gets a little privacy around here. Or is that almost impossible? Then I did weep silently, and holding myself tightly I just felt waves of sadness and desolation and bewilderment wash over and through me. I had these lame pajama things in the bedroll so at some point in that first long and lonely night I slept and thankfully I was alone then, dreaming. Unfamiliar sounds kept waking me up all night, though, and the lights never went out. So even in the dead of night in the middle of the desert, it was never dark; I found this hard to get used to. I would learn that many people had both earplugs and a sleeping mask to deal with the light and almost constant noise of so many people in the same area. Over the next few days I just tried to acclimate myself to this new environment and I was fortunate to have made friends with these women so quickly. They helped me so much. I had to shower, which was a nightmare to me in itself, and change back into the same clothes, since they were all I had. Then Terri gave me some jeans and another shirt of hers to wear and that made a huge difference in how I felt. I had the entire weekend to just get used to being there and the routine that prison was.

I would lie on my bunk many times over that first weekend and just stare at the wall and wonder what had happened to me that I was here, in prison, with the rest of my future complete uncertain, my life in shambles. I would have to figure out what I was doing and right the course of the rest of my life. A few times over the weekend I had been paged to see a counselor and to go to the officer's station for some chore, or probably just to see if I responded and how fast. There were lots of things there that they made you do just because they could, and just to make you do them. Total control issues. I found out about different programs that were available to us, such as "boot camp," where it was like being in the army but if you could hack it for a whole year, you would get a year off your sentence. People did this boot camp and right after, they went off to a halfway house. There was also a 500-hour drug program available. It sounded like something that I could be eligible for. This program also rewarded you with a year off your time. I spoke to the counselor right away about the drug program, determined to get into it as soon as possible. They did not offer it at the Phoenix facility but they had one in Pleasanton, CA and somewhere in Texas and West Virginia. I was going to do everything I could to make this time productive and if there were ways to shorten my sentence, I was going to do them. I also had to arrange to get a job, which I set out to do on Monday. Michelle had told me to go to work for one of the maintenance crews; it was better than the kitchen. So I had to get some form and find the guy at the maintenance office, farther off in back of the prison, towards where the men's prison was located. I talked to this guy and he signed the paper that requested a position with his crew. I had to get that to some other case worker and wait for it to be approved. In the meantime, they finally outfitted me with the hideous prison uniform and let me fill out a form to have some stuff sent to me from my sister. Then they took me outside and put me to work for the rest of the day. The new inmates, and there were a few of us, would be ordered to rake the rocks in this huge area in a certain direction. When we had finished and all the pretty lined were drawn out and it looked nice, they would command you to rake them in another direction. This would go on all day until quitting time. You worked from 7 AM to 4PM, with an hour break for lunch, which was always pretty good, actually.

I was adjusting pretty well, and I was starting to get into the rhythm of the place a little and get down a routine, which is something that you have to have there. A way to feel that you have some of your own order and structure to your life and not just what they want to impose on you. You have to control some aspect of your life so they cannot have it all. I also finally got a commissary card and my money was on it, so as soon as they opened the store, I could take my turn with the others and buy a few things. I also had to pay people back for things that they had loaned to me since I had arrived. You also had to buy phone time. There were no pay phones or anything. The money went into a phone account and you were given a personal way to access it. If you didn't have money in this account, you did not make phone calls. I put fifty dollars in it so I could call my sister and my mom as soon as I was allowed. I had no plan to call Richie from here; anyway, you had to have your phone list approved. Same with anyone that might come to visit you. You had to fill out forms and they had to be approved. It would take several days, normally, so even if you finally had money in your account, if you had an unapproved list, you still were not making any calls. Writing to people was not as hard, but if they were like Joe, one of your co-defendants or whatever, they had to approve that too. I was trying to get permission to correspond with Joe from the start. I loved Richie, but I loved Joe, too, and he was in the same boat as me, having to survive the loneliness and the hardships of prison and I just felt more connected to him for that. I also figured that Richie should do the best he could to just start his life over again, fresh and clean without the pressures of a girlfriend in jail. I did not want him sending me money, just to take care of himself and get on with his life. This felt right to me. I loved him but I had to deal with this, now, and it was easier without talking to him. But I really wanted to know that Joe was all right and doing okay, wherever he was.

Life settled into a prison routine. I got the new job and started following a woman named Sally around, since she was leaving soon and she did all the plumbing and repairs on the washers and dryers. I would be learning her job and taking her place on the crew. Amazingly enough, I had an aptitude for this work and before long she was just watching me do everything. This was a very good feeling; and it really boosted my self-esteem about just how true it was that I could do anything if I set my mind, will and energies to accomplish it, or learn it. I became surprisingly proficient and everything at that camp ran like clockwork. All of us women, for the most part, worked hard and the pay was just ludicrous. I was making 12 cents an hour when I started. Once I took over Sally's job, I was up to 17 cents. The most I ever made, as the second lead on the crew, was 23 cents an hour. If your family or friends were not sending you any money while you were away, you would really suffer. Like anywhere else, it made a huge difference to your comfort levels if you were being taken care of while you were there. You could buy your own food and clothes and makeup and coffee and smokes and all kinds of things, like decent shampoo and toothpaste. There is so much that you take for granted that you have to just give up when you go to prison.

But to do anything was an ordeal. I had to see the case manager so many times to try to get into the drug program. Because I had a state conviction, also, they had something called a detainer against me, and until that was lifted they could not put me on the list. But as far as rehabilitation goes, the system is a joke from what I could and would see. There are so few programs or anything, even in the federal system, to actually give you new skills or a new chance. That's what this whole system of justice is trying to accomplish, right? I guess you could say I was least learning how to be an apprentice plumber. It was kind of great because I usually went off by myself and fixed stuff. There would be other people around, but sometimes there was actually no one around at all. I would just work very slowly and take my time and milk it, or it would take me awhile because my first attempt to fix it did not work.

One day the customs guy, Steve, that I had worked with, and Rick, the FBI guy, came out to the prison to see me. I went up to the office when they called me, wondering what the hell was up that they were calling me there. You hardly ever got called there. I went in and there they were and we went to talk in an office, alone. They were asking how I was and expressing their personal regret that I was there at all, because of all I had done for them; they saw no reason at all for me to even be in prison. Well, that's just great to hear, but here I am. I thanked them, though, and they started talking about the possibility of trials and testifying and I told them about this detainer thing that I had on me because of the state case that no one made go away and was now hurting me, because of this drug program, etc. They said that they would look into it for me and see if there was anything they could do. I told them, hey, it's a year off and aside from this detainer, I qualify for it. Please try to help me. They said they would be in touch, and they left, and I sneaked out of the office, hoping no one had seen me talking to two dudes who looked like feds. Well, it was either them or I don't know what, but at some point during the next several months, I was interviewed to enter the program and be transferred to whichever place they wanted. I told them I preferred to be sent to Pleasanton, but I just wanted the program and if there was another place, I would go there instead. It was looking good for me to be leaving by that August, or so.

I was running every day, no matter how hot it was, just running around the track, around and around. I would run at least 5 miles every day. I was also going to the Jehovah's Witness meetings with Penny and Terri, to whom I had become much closer. They were good people and I was actually doing pretty well with my routines. Working, running, writing letters, making phone calls, reading a lot of books, eating at the designated times, making our own coffee. After awhile you just fall into patterns, and you adapt. I am very adaptable, and it was not that hard, at a decent place like this one, to get into the swing of things and be good and not get in trouble.

If you did things wrong, they would write you up and it was on your record. The drug program for instance: if you had been written up and been problematic, you weren't getting in. I kept to myself and hung with my little circle of friends and a few other people I talked to, and laid low. I was enjoying the Bible study with the Jehovah's Witness couple that came to the prison. They were very nice to us. I was really listening and not scoffing; I needed a higher Power to help me in my times of need. No matter how well I was coping and getting along most of the time, there were many times where I went in search of a private spot, maybe out in the field by the running track, or some other semi-isolated spot, and I could cry, quietly, crouched down trying to hide from the rest of the community I lived in. It was something that I just needed to do. There was a certain amount of pent-up sorrow and loneliness and it had to be released. Around my friends, I tried to be lively and fun-loving, and we did have a lot of good times, even there. It was fairly cushy, for prison, and we enjoyed whatever they had to offer.

My mom and my sister came to see me one weekend. It was wonderful to see them. I had never had a visitor before, besides the agents, and it was really great to go out to the patio area of the visiting room and hang out for most of the day, talking. It was horrible to say goodbye, however, and I almost thought that it would be better to get no visits and just not deal with the fact that you can't leave. I felt awful for my mom; she was so miserable when they had to leave and it was difficult to watch them go. It was quite depressing too, after they left. I sat on my bunk, or lay facing the wall, my form of privacy (all of ours), and think about what my life was and what did I intend to do about it?

I always had a calendar and I counted down the days. Big "X's" over each day that passed and a small number counting down from 1278 days. That quickly became too much and I stopped the counting until there were better numbers coming up. I was finally given permission to write to Joe and we began corresponding with each other. It was so wonderful to be communicating with him and talking of love and togetherness again. It really helped get me through the days. Looking forward to a letter or a phone call to make is the highlight of your life there, besides a visit, of course. But that's it. Everything else is routine and the perks are limited, as I suppose they should be. We were in prison for crimes we allegedly committed, after all. Why should we be rewarded for that? I respected that and was grateful for all the comforts that the camp did have.

Days just blur into one another. There are minor conflicts, like with the job, but as with any job, there are always annoying people and this was just intensified because we were in prison. Some of the chicks on my crew, for example, were just really rough around the edges and it was uncomfortable to have to work with them, but you did because you had to and I tried to be as cool and distant as possible. Detached. We did a huge project at the men's prison and built this huge wall. Then we started another major job and built the new commissary for our camp. We really worked. But we had a lot of pride in our work and definitely (for the most part) took it seriously and we did a damn good job! I was pretty proud of myself for all the hard physical work I was doing. I am grateful for that experience, and I think, over all, that this kind of camps are much more healthy and prone to build self-esteem and working with others, etc. than some prison that locks you up in cages and promotes a negative attitude of tension and hostility and isolation. I was one of the lucky ones who could go to such a place. First time, non-violent, female, white-collar crime, even though it was drug-related. The actual federal charge I was convicted of was in fact conspiracy to launder money; the state conviction was the charge of conspiracy with intent to possess and distribute marijuana, over 500 lbs — when, in fact, that whole state charge was for the marijuana and money that we had planted in all those various storage units and actually turned in to state cops and the feds for Rudy's case. The charges were totally bogus. But since I never got charged for the warehouse full of marijuana in Staten Island that they knew I had rented and facilitated, and no one in Arizona had ever charged me with anything . . . All in all, I felt like I had been bruised by the system, but was something that I could live with, given all the things that I had done that I have never been caught for.

Payback is a bitch. I believe that what comes around goes around and that everything happens for a reason. Not that I had always believed that — but I had come to, and I was looking for the lessons I needed to get out of this. I had created this experience in my life and I wanted, needed, to under-stand why. I spent a lot of time pondering these things, and my perception of deity and deep personal things and talking about them through writing and receiving letters from Joe. We had gotten very close again and he was having a bad time in prison. Because of his weapons charge (from what seemed like so long ago), he was in a medium-security prison and had to totally watch his ass 24/7. Life was not good for him and I felt so guilty about that. He was very happy that I was in a place that was pretty decent and minimum secu-rity was definitely where it was at. I had a feeling that it was really bad for Joe in there but that he was not going to tell me that and worry me. His heart is true.

All of us (Terri, Penny, Michelle and I) were trying to get into the drug program. Penny could not get in for at least another year — her sentence was a year longer than Terri's and that was part of the thing, too. The amount of time you had left. Their plan was that you got into the program for the last year of your time and went almost directly from completing the 500-hour program to a six month halfway house. It was looking real good for both Terri and me to get the program starting that September. We talked about that a lot, and it was definitely something to work for. So with that kind of motivation and my own personal motivation to truly know myself and learn and change and grow while I was there, I had this time to reflect and start taking control of the direction of my life.

After awhile, living there, the daily routine gets very familiar and you just slip into a semi-trance and just go about your half-life. I ran every night, and sometimes it was 110 degrees out there at nine o'clock. Take a shower and go to bed to read the Bible, usually, and work on the Watchtower material that I was studying. I was still immensely enjoying the biblical education I was getting and the approval from the Witness couple. Penny and Terri knew a lot more than me; they were fairly knowledgeable when I was just learning. It was hard for them because they were lesbians and obviously the Bible does not condone, but in fact condemns homosexuals and it was understood that for them to ever have any standing in the church, they could not be gay. But still they studied and I really admired and respected that; and so did the couple who taught us, who never would say a bad word about any of us. It was a welcome visit every Sunday afternoon to spend an hour with them talking about Jehovah and Bible passages and what it all meant to us and how we should live and behave to please God. I did not agree with everything that I was learning, but I really respected these kind people and I appreciated their time and energy, their efforts to teach of their god and their ways. I also was keeping an open mind and taking everything in, spending a lot of time praying and trying to feel this god Jehovah in my life and heart. It was suddenly very important that I have some deeper and meaningful sense of the Divine and a relationship with Deity.

I was working hard at becoming more aware and compassionate. The only problem with it all was that, in my heart, my truth is Pagan. I still studied the beliefs of the Witnesses and the Bible and its content. If we knew that definite parts were not true or accurate, how could we live with it as a guide? I prayed more and did start to feel a deeper connection, but the energy always felt feminine in nature and I did not feel that it was this god, Jehovah, but some Other that I had known before but forgotten. I kept these things to myself and prayed to She Who was Hidden. There were no pagan groups but lots of Christian ones. I was developing my intuition as well. I was almost completely relying on my gut, my inner wisdom, my instincts to interact with people every day and to choose my friends wisely. I was moving forward in ways I was not even aware of. I was experiencing growth, so the experience was proving to be valuable and I could really be productive about exploring myself, spirituality, growth, change, inner strength and respect. Most days, I was okay, and then you just have those days where nothing seemed to lift your spirits and you are just looking at this bleak reality of prison and ludicrously low paying jobs and confinement. I had lots of time to wrestle with inner demons, so I got started. I figured that the drug program would tackle some issues and would be a beneficial and worth-while investment of time.

I had been there almost eight months by now and it was late July and really hot. Both Terri and I received word that we would be leaving Phoenix to go to the drug program. I was going to Pleasanton and Terri was off to the West Virginia place. Bummer. It would have been really great to have been transported with a friend — because it was a nightmare. I was so jazzed to be leaving, not understanding what it was like to be moved from one facility to another. I said my goodbyes, as did Terri and the few others who were leaving. People were always coming and going. There were people there with sentences from as little as three months to 15 years.

Anyway, they came to me in mid August of 1996 and took me away, and into the front offices where you come in. I was made to change into way too big khaki prison transport clothes. Then I was shackled up, completely. Ankle and wrist shackles, chains around my waist that linked to the wrist shackles. I had to just stand around like that, feeling simply horrified to be chained up like this, until the van arrived that would take me away. I was the only one going to Pleasanton, and I was all alone for this one. Another test.

That was what I had begun to think; that all these difficult but challenging and interesting situations that I had created for myself were tests of my inner strength, resolve, courage, integrity, purity, heart. Even as I dreaded this one, I tried to harden my heart enough to make it through whatever was to come during this transport from Phoenix to northern California. It was yet another situation where I had absolutely no clue what was going to happen to me and there was simply not one damn thing that I could do about any of it. It was having to utterly surrender to people, situations and whatever these might throw at you. And you had to just take it. We made a stop at an airport somewhere out in the desert and more women got on. We drove, mostly in silence, for awhile and we finally arrived at a larger airport. I glimpsed a lot of activity around some of the planes and when I got a clearer look, I could see that there were lines of shackled men, all linked together with more chains and all over the place were dudes with rifles, big guns pointed at all the prisoners.

I was told to get out and, shambling along, trying to walk in the ankle shackles, we proceeded to the area where all the convicts and sharpshooters were. Here was another of those times where I surveyed an unreal scene before me and I just cried to myself, can I go back now? I changed my mind . . . the hell with this drug program, let's just drive back to Phoenix. It was like some scene out of a bad movie and I thought, these people do this everyday! I got used to standing there with 20 rifles pointed straight at me. There was just me and a few other women waiting to get on one of the planes, a tiny minority to all the men that were waiting. I thought that this would be a real different kind of plane ride than I was used to. After standing for I don't know how long, we (the chained link I was attached to) were told to board the plane. This was much more difficult, since the planes were on the ground and we had to climb the steep steps. Let me tell you, climbing was not easy. When your ankles are shackled, as well as the waist and wrist, you can barely move and your sense of balance is disturbed. I took my time despite their commands to "move along" and "hurry up." I was not going to fall on my ass in front of all these people. They kind of shove you towards a seat and you sit down — which is hard, too, with no freedom of movement. More people (men) kept getting on the plane until it was stuffed with 99% guys and a handful of us forlorn girls. The guys were scary; leering and making suggestive noises if they caught your eye or even thought that they might be noticed. I felt like a piece of meat being herded from one place to another. There was no regard for our comfort and when the time came after we had taken off that I unfortunately had to go to the bathroom. This was a whole new nightmare. Shuffling down the tiny aisle was bad enough, but when you add into the account the very real and disturbing fact that there were 200 men trying to grab you as you shuffled by, and the comments, and expressions on their poor faces. Even though all I could see of them was that they were all desperate, I felt the same sorrow and compassion for them that I felt for myself. I also understood their need to perform, to put on some kind of show for their buddies and the guards. That did not make it any easier to get to the stupid bathroom and somehow shut the door. Then I was immediately confronted with the next problem: how perform this task; I could not figure out how I was going to get these stupid pants down with my wrists all shackled to pee into the toilet! Ah . . . It seems so simple when we do this four-five times a day. Try to do it now with your hands bound. I think that the only thing that saved me was the fact that the pants were so big on me. I started moving around and somehow tugging down the pants by kind of hopping and managed after quite awhile to get them down far enough that I could just pee. I sat down and choked back sobs again. This was just too much. After I relieved myself, there was the new dilemma of getting the pants back up. For some reason, this turned out to be a little easier than getting them down had been. Then the long, torturous shuffle back to my seat. I did not even dare look around at all the men I could feel staring at me. I would not get up again, no matter what.

I did not even know where we were going. You just do whatever they tell you. This is obviously why there are so many people who become institutionalized. (Like good convicts) they get used to being directed when and where to do everything in their lives. Some who are inside long enough simply seem to lose even the will to make their own decisions. It is much easier to just do nothing and let others tell you what to do. It's very sad and it is the fault of the system, and not the felon, for this occurring at all. It's a crime in itself, to strip another human being of all dignity and self respect, to the point that they no longer even have urges to make their own choices or decide things for themselves. If they are released, they wind up right back inside, because the "real" world is literally too hard for them to cope with anymore. They now need an environment where their every move and activity is directed and they actually feel comfortable with this "known" community. I was fervently praying that I would be once again dropped off at some airport with more armed dudes everywhere and placed in another van and driven to this prison camp in Pleasanton.

Well, since that sounds simple, we can assume that this was not what happened. It made sense and would have been too easy. When the plane finally landed, we were all taken off and it appeared that we were at a large facility. I would come to find out that it was like a transport station for human cargo, criminals; we would have to be checked out here and stay until another flight going in the right direction was leaving. I wanted to scream and panic again. How long would I be here? I heard stories of people being here for months on end because some BOP moron had lost their paperwork. This was a real jail. The energy was intense. I wound up being thrown into a cell, yes, a cell, with the door clanging shut behind me and locked. This was not good.

The plane ride was really short and in no time I was in a van and cruising down some northern California highway towards my new home. Same deal, minimum security, federal prison work camp. I figured that I would just keep doing the plumbing thing (if they needed one) and focus on the drug program. I had heard that just a few years earlier, this camp had actually been co-ed. That would have made things more interesting. I was really glad that it was not. I had enough to distract me from my goals during this time in prison. Who needed the added pressures of men all over the place? Dealing with all these women was enough for me. I was utterly miserable that long afternoon and evening. Time seemed to completely stop and there were a lot of women all over the place and lots of noise and curses and laughter and shouting. The din was unnerving and I was a wreck. How could Joe stand it? I felt indescribably degraded by all that had happened in only a few hours. I was so low. I just laid there and was not hungry and I just wanted to die. It's very fortunate for me that I was sent to minimum security, with the openness and illusion of freedom. I would not have made it if I had been locked up for my whole sentence. The night was endless and I tormented myself as I lay awake and sick at heart, feeling absolutely that I was this tiny less-than-a-grain of sand being compared to the Infinite Universe, and what did my personal pain and strength mean in the scheme of things, anyway? Once I get morose and depressed, watch out. It was a miserable night and I wondered constantly if I would be leaving in the morning. Please, I prayed, let me be told to get up and get out of here! I think I may have slept a couple of hours total, fitful, shaky, dis-eased sleep. I was awake again when the noise in the bleak place started to escalate. Oh, it must mean it's morning. I was completely disoriented. I did not know what time it was and what was going to happen to me and I just continued to lay there miserably, awaiting whatever was in store for me today. I actually thought about the Phoenix prison longingly, and I imagined Terri having to go through this same nightmarish experience just to get to another institution. I mentally sent her love and strength and this action made me feel better, too. Stronger, a little less defeated. I silently thanked She Who was Hidden, and when a guard came around and said that we could leave the cell, I went in search of a cigarette, which I was dying for, and maybe some breakfast? Being a way-station, the place was teeming with women being moved for whatever reason. Seeing them and feeling the energy present at this place made me want to scream and crawl under a rock and hide. I had to get out of here, today. I worked in my mind to make it be so and after a few hours had passed and I had bummed several cigarettes, the guards started calling out numbers and last names to begin to move people into areas for transportation out. I heard my number and name and gave a silent whoop of elation in my head and moved quickly over to the area they wanted me to be in. The process from the day before was then repeated: All the cuffs, shackles and chains were attached to me again, but this time I did not care or flinch. I just wanted to leave and they could truss me up like a goddamned turkey and haul me out upside down on a stick, just let me leave. The entire experience that had so unnerved me the day before was no big deal today, and all I wanted to do was to get to Pleasanton.

As we drove up to the camp, there were women hanging out in front, in a woodsy looking area, like a small park with benches and grass. Pretty. Everyone was staring and waiting for the van. New people are always an interesting diversion from the doldrums of daily prison life. You get out of the van, looking like a mass murderer in your shackles and transport clothes and feeling debased. They herded me and the two other women into an office and we did the strip search thing again, which is always humiliating and degrading, no matter how many times you do it. Same with peeing in a cup, which we again had to do every time they demanded it. They are practically breathing down your neck while you try to urinate and I, for one, cannot pee on command and it's very hard for me to do so at all when some bitch is in my face. I never got used to that. Not even after five years of having to do it.

Then we met with a train wreck of a woman, a counselor at the camp. She was one scary bitch and of course, she wound up being my personal counselor while I was living there and I would have to deal with this unpredictable woman throughout my delightful stay at Pleasanton. Back to the present.

After more paperwork, this woman told me that I would not get into the drug program next month, whereupon I just asked, well, then why was I sent here? Send me back. I was sick of being treated like a piece of dirt and after this harrowing and upsetting move here, I was not going to listen to some bullying prison matron tell me I was not getting the program. Damn! Didn't any of these idiots know what the other was doing? I tried to not let my hungry mind attack this new possibility of no drug program and go crazy with it. Hard to do.

After all of this festive fun, we were taken to a building (they were all old-looking, nothing like the newness of Phoenix), and led inside. It was where we would be living for awhile. It was set up like one huge room with bunk beds and there was absolutely no privacy whatsoever and looked like some horrible army set-up. I was again just knocked over. My head was screaming that I couldn't live like this and I was devastated that I had ever left Phoenix by this point. Everything I had seen and experienced since leaving was worse than anything that had ever happened to me there. Or, at least, that's what it felt like at this stage. I again choked back sobs of unhappiness and utter misery and tried to act like this was no big deal. I wound up on a top bunk with a very rude and hostile black woman on the bottom. Every time I even slightly moved on the top, she would bitch that I was shaking the whole bed and I began to get angry, even though I feared her — she was big and looked like she could and would seriously hurt me. I was sick and tired over the last two days of taking all of this abuse and I was not going to continue to be treated with no respect, especially by some big ugly convict. She was probably just as miserable and scared and confused as me, but she was being rude, so I got down and got back in her face, saying she had just better chill out.

This whole acclimation thing was hard enough to deal with and her attitude was not helping. Fortunately, most of the other women surrounding my immediate area were pleasant enough and I ignored the negative woman entirely. In a closely populated community such as ours, that was essentially all you could do with "bad" people; do your best to avoid them and ignore them if for any reason you cannot. I could not even turn my head one way or the other on the bunk to try to pretend I had privacy, as there were beds and women everywhere. The bathrooms were really awful and with my new plumber's eye I saw so much broken equipment everywhere, I figured they sure as hell needed me here. Toilets, sinks and showers were broken, making it that much more stressful to all live here together. I saw lots more petty arguments here then I had in Phoenix. They had a nice running track, though, and that cheered me. But once again being the new fish, I would have to wait days for the camp uniforms to be issued to me (at least they had a much cooler set of uniforms to work in here) and for the box of my personal things to get here from Phoenix. I had to go through the whole paperwork thing again, along with the phone list of people I wanted to call and the visiting list that all had to be approved before I could make a phone call or write to anyone, not to mention receive mail, which is the highlight of a normal prison day. To get mail is heaven. Everybody goes to mail call. If for some reason you can't, you make sure that someone goes for you. It's the only time, besides getting a visit, where it's fun to hear your number being called. Every other time it's usually something bad or at the very least unpleasant.

In spite of my low-grade horror over this new place and my living arrangements, I got productive and started finding out some of the things I would need to know. Who was in charge of the maintenance crew here? How could I apply to work for him? I made an appointment to see that rude counselor woman and to get this drug program thing straightened out and to find out when it started. I had also found out that there were rooms that women lived in here, four ladies to a room. The rooms had doors with no locks and it was just a room with two sets of bunk beds on either side and four lockers and a desk with a window looking out into the walkway between buildings. It looked pretty good to me after seeing this dormitory style of living that I was going to have to cope with for however long. I also found out that the people that were in the current drug program all lived together in one of the buildings and that they were all getting ready to leave. This year's class was almost over and most of them would be going to halfway houses. Regardless, that bunch of rooms was reserved for the next drug class, the one that I had better be in. So I probably wouldn't be moving until they vacated the building. I wondered how long that would be. Living in this military building was a real drain on my morale. I really tried to not be there and of course I just started running again. Round and round. The food was pretty good and once again, quickly enough for the adaptable chameleon that I am, I was adjusting to the place, the women, the guards and the living arrangements, along with the new fears, doubts and uncertainties that went along wherever I went.

I started working as a plumber and there was tons for me to do and I stayed really busy for awhile working all over the camp and repairing stuff that had been broken — and broken for quite some time, from all appearances. Lots of people liked me because of this. More people could take a shower or wash something in the sinks or go to the bathroom once everything was working properly, and maintained by me, too. The foreman of the crew was a jerk, but some of the other guys that we worked with were all right. I settled back into the old routines, and once again started receiving my mail. My package came and I could finally wear my own jeans and t-shirts again when I wasn't made to wear the prison clothes. I also hooked up with the Jehovah's Witnesses. I missed talking about spiritual things with nice people from outside and even if I did not agree with everything, it was all I had and I wanted to do more. I was also taking a correspondence course in accounting that I had started in Phoenix and I was almost done. It was just a cheesy diploma, but I was proud of myself for finishing it. I ran a lot and I was in excellent shape. I was eating pretty healthy and I was barely smoking anymore. I was doing good things for my body, mind and soul while I waited to get out of prison. I consoled myself with this kind of thought. Writing to Joe again was fantastic as well. I would write 20-page letters every couple of days and receive beautiful, and lengthy replies. Writing letters is a major occupation of time and you can almost get rid of the rest of the world by putting on your trusty walkman and lying on your bunk, or sitting somewhere outside when the weather is nice, and just writing page after page of feelings and love and longing. These letters kept me going when nothing else worked. I could be at the bottom for whatever reason that being in prison provoked, and I would just get out one of his letters and read it again, over and over, and my heart would lift like a hawk in the jet stream and I could go on. I would find whatever it was I needed to do so deep inside and take a deep breath and go on. Tackling the spiritual issues of the Witnesses also was a stimulating and very meaningful preoccupation that I derived great pleasure from doing. I would spend hours pouring over the Watchtowers and reading the Bible, not once, but twice, completely. I was also spending a lot of time praying in my heart to She Who was Hidden, not that I was terribly conscious of it, because for the most part, I was not.

I spoke with my mom, dad, Ben in New Jersey, my sister, and once in awhile, Joe's mom, as often as I could afford to call. They all would send money from time to time and it is only because of my family's and friends' generosity, love and compassion for me that I lived well in prison. They took care of me. When you make 17 cents an hour, your paycheck is not going to buy you much at all. Ben kept asking me if I would consider coming back to NJ when this was over. I was simply irreplaceable and wonderful (blush) and his business was growing and he would always need someone who could do so much, blah, blah. He was sincere and I knew he meant it. I just could not even dream of ever going back to New Jersey, where all of this had happened, at least in my head. I was going to be with Joe, though. That was what we were talking about and it's all that I wanted. I still thought about Richie a lot, as well. I wondered how he was getting along and I hoped that he was well and happy. I just never envisioned a future with him once I went away and he went into witness protection. I loved him, but I felt that our separation had also happened for a reason and that it would be better for both of us if we just kept going in our own lives. Everything with Joe and me was in the same category, in my mind: it was happening for a reason. Everything that we had been through together and the fact that we were once again so close even at this distance and in these prisons, and it felt like Joe and I were still in love, deeply, and ready to do this as best we could and be together once again. This kept me looking forward to the next day, and the next. Without these wellsprings of hope, it is nearly impossible to live and try to be happy in prison. You gotta have something to cling to. It's imperative to your survival and emotional well-being.

I finally somehow untangled the mess of my entrance into the 500-hour drug program and those of us who were getting in started moving out of the awful military dormitory, or other housing units they may have been residing in. This same unpleasant counselor woman was the one who was deciding who would be in what rooms with whom. Here were the four-women rooms, and there were only 24 of us entering the program, six rooms. I wound up being one of the last people this lady even considered, so I found myself moving into a room with people I had never met before and whose energies did not strike me as promising. Three (sorry, but it's true) sullen black women and me: a little honky hard rock chick. I would find out that one of them was a nice person, and even the others could be real and interesting at times; but the whole vibe I got from all of them when I moved into the room was that I was dirt, they ruled, and I had better just toe the line with them. Great. I saw another test taking shape in my life and decided to apply Christian principles to all that I did in my relationships and try to understand and empathize. I had to live with these people in a tiny room! We all worked and were in and out of the room, but for something like writing at the desk (which I had totally been looking forward to), I would never have a chance since one of them was always there. I was last in line.

Once in awhile, they would all be gone and I could just be alone for awhile; that was luxurious and pure heaven.

I had actual conversations with them and tried to get to know them and not judge them. I couldn't avoid them. It worked, for the most part, and we began an uneasy yet harmonious enough co-existence. I was real tolerant and forgiving of most things and I tried to be that way as much as I could. When they got to be too awful, which they did plenty of times, I would put on my walkman and blast hard rock into my ears and drown them out entirely, in my own world. That was a great blessing. I was also making other friends with some of the other women next door, or one down the hall, and I would also find other places to go. They liked to watch TV and I never watched TV in prison. It was a hassle and certain people just ruled it and it was stupid so I did not even bother to try. I would rather study the Bible or read or write letters or run.

The drug program officially commenced in late September and we met the guy who would be our teacher for the next year. He deserves better, but I've forgotten his name at the moment. If I get it I will let you know. He was really a wonderful man and I really grew fond of him and I know that he liked me a lot as well. I was one of the handful of women who took the course seriously and really tried to learn and get something out of it. For ourselves. Not just the year off, and from what I saw of most of these people, they were just going to sit there for the next year to lessen their sentence.

He interviewed us all personally before we started the 500 hours and I liked him from the start. I decided that I would shine in this course and would really be an active participant and contribute as much as I could to the positive energies that may or may not exist. He would badger some of these listless bodies that attended the class and try to get something out of them. Or we would ignore them and about six of us would be into it and really get talking about something. The thing I loved the most about the whole program was the content, and I think they should be doing this in every prison in the country, especially if they are going to keep locking so many people up. The entire thrust of this drug program was about cognitive thinking. Not about how much dope did you shoot up, but on the theories of the thought patterns predetermining our behaviors, as what we think is how we feel. I loved this concept and felt its truth and dug in wholeheartedly to doing this course well and thoroughly. We met several times a week, after work, in our own building for about 2 hours. This would go on for the next year. It was a great stimulating addition to the prison routine for me and I looked forward to the classes, even when you would be talking with some chick who wasn't into it and would act like it was a drag. I was actually keeping very busy and, on cold winter nights, the little room with the four of us in it would be cozy and toasty. You could buy flannels and stuff to wear and everyone wore these things all the time. Life went on.

Little things mean a lot there, and can change your entire mood and attitude for the good or bad. Everyone was like this so there are times when you are walking on eggshells with people because they just were on the phone and got bad news from home, or something. A depressing letter from a boyfriend. A bad day at work. Just depressed, in general. Lots of women were on meds and they would go to pill call every day, or twice a day. Probably due to the stress of the move and the atmosphere upon my arrival, my face had broken out horribly; terrible cystic acne attacked my poor face. It made me feel dreadful, ugly; and they were painful, too. Like cysts on my face and along my jawline. It got so I could barely sleep with the giant one along my jaw, and finally after several trips to the prison doctor, I got the guy to prescribe me something strong: Acutaine, which I will endorse here gratefully. It saved my life and started to work pretty quickly. I began to feel better about my poor face and appearance and that raised my spirits. This was several months in coming though. Everything in prison is dragged out and takes forever to make happen.

It was now late May of 1997 and I was actually starting to think about getting out. My calendar once again had days counted down and I was looking at leaving in early September. I had been a very good girl in prison. I never had been written up or gotten into any trouble at all. I actually acted as a Witness in prison and talked to people about Jehovah and Jesus, and served them. I learned about service to the Gods from studying with the Witnesses. I am very grateful for that and I consider it time very well spent. I had actually been fired from my job, mainly (!) because everything was fixed and they didn't know what to do with me. I had to do the kitchen thing for a little while, which was dreadful, but then I hooked up with the most bitchen job at the camp, for the elite chicks that could be trusted. It entailed working outside the camp every day, driving in a van to San Francisco and working with Forest and Parks services doing a variety of things, from painting miles of curbs to painting bathrooms along the beach (!) to going into the forests (!) and clearing deadwood all day and then shredding it in the machines. It was totally awesome and it was incredible to get out every day of the work week and see the beach or the trees in the forest or just normal people in their cars. It was a great drive to and from, every day, too. We of course had to wear our prison garb but it wasn't that bad and the Parks Services people were always so totally nice to us. We had a driver too, one woman guard who was so cool and would take us for drives, and we would get out and look over cliffs at the water and it was magnificent. We all felt special every night when we came back to the camp and got out of the van. There was only about six of us and several of them were my friends. It was very fortunate that I was given this opportunity.

I was so excited the days before I was leaving that nothing could bum me out. The day came and I was packed and ready and I had to walk across the street to another building where I would be officially released from prison for five whole days. It was amazing. I was ecstatic, beyond words. I was going to be free for five days! Not in prison! I will never forget the beautiful elation that I felt. It seemed like all of this good was being rewarded in beautiful ways and I was grateful and hopeful and ready to start a new life with Joe, whom I loved more than ever. It opened up another wonderful opportunity as well. I was being seriously considered for a five day furlough! Out of the prison! This happened fairly frequently here and I was thinking it was definitely going to happen for me, too. I was doing everything right, and it was no act. I was totally excelling at their drug program which was nearing its conclusion, and I had the most "I can be trusted" job in the place. It happened. My mom arranged to fly in and we would go and stay near Fremont, CA where Joe was now living with his mom. Joe had just recently gotten out of prison and had been briefly in a halfway house before he could move back into his mom's house for awhile and get on his feet again. It was awesome. Now I had permission to talk to him on the phone in addition to the letters we still wrote constantly. Long letters. Everything seemed perfect between us and it was a big part of my furlough that I was going to get to see him and we could spend time together and talk about the future and make love!!!

The first thing that my mom and I did when we drove away was to go and get a real breakfast at Coco's, where I ordered the eggs benedict, and was looking around me in wonder and a childlike joy. It was mighty fine to be outside again, doing whatever I wanted. The food tasted so good I was just beside myself. My mom was so happy to see me so relaxed and we were just having a wonderful time. It was simply an incredibly beautiful northern California day and the wind whipped my hair and I reveled in the feelings of freedom with joy. I had been out, of course, a lot because of my job, but this was completely different and I appreciated it so much. We drove to the motel room and just hung out and talked and ate and I was so happy to be there and I was pinching myself and could not believe that this was really happening. Every time that reality part of my brain would pop in and announce that I would be going back in approximately 112 hours, I would shut it up and live in the wonderful moment I was in.

I talked to Joe on the phone, in the same town, and we arranged to see each other the very next day. He sounded subdued, and I did not know why, but I was too excited to dwell on anything that wasn't positive and adding to my joy at being free. I slept like a log in the quiet room, with no rapping black women yapping the night away. I felt fantastic when we arrived at Joe's house and went up to the door. I was nervous, though. It had been about three years now since I had seen him in jail. Would he look the same? Feel the same? Love me the same? I had hundreds of pages of loving letters to prove that he would, but still I was apprehensive. He was my love!

He came out and there he was! It was awesome and I went to him and hugged him gently. He still seemed a little subdued and I wondered again what might have happened to him in prison and what he was thinking about. I did not totally know him anymore. I thought I did, from all the letters and then the calls, but things are different in person sometimes. I hugged his mom, and she and my mom talked for awhile, and then Joe and I left. We were going to get some sandwiches and go to a secluded creek that he knew of in the forest and we could talk and stuff. He had not attempted to kiss me or touch me or anything. I was kind of just being quiet, not sensing any of the passion and love that he had written and spoken of. We stopped and got the sandwiches and we were talking, but not that much; and he drove us to a beautiful, woodsy place where we got out and walked down until I could see the creek and he led us to a cool spot by the water and we sat down and ate. I was hungry and it was good and it seemed to help him out as well. He became more animated and playful, the Joe I knew and loved so much, and we stripped and got into the water. There were plenty of spots where we could swim and play. It was a little cold but felt simply exquisite on my skin and my psyche. It had been so long since I had been immersed in natural spring water. So pure and cleansing.

He was suddenly amorous and familiar with me and we were finally kissing and holding each other tightly and passionately and we made love in the clean water and it was wonderful. It had been quite a while since I had made love. Him too, I guess. He was ready, now, to talk. I figured that making love to him would break the ice between us. But what he had to say was devastating to me. He did not think that I should come out here when I was released, after all. He needed time and he also thought that the authorities would scrutinize us if we got together right away, and I should maybe just go and live in Colorado with my mom for awhile and we could see how things went and decide then.

Well, I am not going to get into my whole reaction to this but I respected what he was saying nevertheless, and I told him that. I loved him, wanted him to be happy and feel comfortable, and I did not want to add any pressure to whatever stress he was already facing. I really felt that way, though my heart was weighing heavy with sorrow. But being in prison, I could hide this sorrow away to experience and explore later, and try to have a great time while I was still with him. It was not that he did not love me, just did not want to resume our relationship as it had been, when I got out. I had to live with his decision and I would make other plans instead. We wound up leaving there and went to another place where we played, and talked; and it was so good to be with him again, no matter how brief it would be. All in all, I had a beautiful time and he brought me back to the motel room where my mom was hanging out, waiting for me. Me and mom were going to do some stuff the next day, going to the Monterey aquarium and driving around, which we both loved. Joe came in for a little while and he was being sweet and wonderful and oh, how I loved him. I was so happy and so sad. I would see him the day after tomorrow, again, the day before I had to go back to the camp. The rest of the furlough was just as great.

My mom and I had a wonderful time the next day and Joe and I had a great visit as well the next. I felt fantastic and happy to be with him. But nothing was changed; so I told him that I was going to think about what he had said and I would be changing the location of the halfway house I expected to go to. You have to plan all of that stuff out six months in advance. They wouldn't like it that I was changing at this late date. Too bad. If he did not want me there, I was not going to be there.

My mom drove me back to the prison and I got out with my little bag and fiercely hugged her goodbye. I would be leaving in a few months now, but it had been a great time of closeness for us and it was so hard to say goodbye. I know it was nearly impossible for her to have to let me go back in. That was what I had to do, however. I walked back inside and she drove away. Strip search again, and urine test, make sure I wasn't getting high on dope the whole time I was gone. Hate these degrading experiences of total submission and violation upon my person. Grimly submitted to them. The rest of the time passed quickly in the routines of life there and the excitement of leaving. I was awarded an honorary certificate from the drug program for excellent contributions or something and that was very gratifying. I had enjoyed the class and the time spent and felt like I had benefited from the entire experience and I did not regret it happening to me anymore. I did not like it, but I was not thinking that this entire length of time had been wasted, either. I thought a lot about where I should go, what I should do now. I thought a lot about going to my mom's, but it did not feel like the right thing to do. I was 35 years old. I couldn't go to my mom's. I thought a lot about what Ben had said and wondered if I should indeed go back to New Jersey (ye gods) and work for him and get my real life back together again. It was an assured job and that was a big deal for me now; I was a convicted felon and that wasn't going away, ever. To have someone who already respected you and your abilities, appreciated you, and actually loved you (because he does) to work for after this experience would be very good. So I talked to Ben about it. I had to make a decision, and fast. The case manager was going to have a fit when I told her that I was changing my release information.

Ben was very supportive and enthusiastic about my coming there. He was thrilled I was considering this. He would help me out 100% and would do whatever he could to lessen the pressures of the halfway house, whatever those would be. I was so touched and felt so appreciated. I told him that I was coming. I would be there on September 4th. I would call him when I could from the halfway house over that first weekend and I would come to work on Monday. I was starting to get excited myself to go there. It was a chance at a decent job without a struggle and a great friend who would help me get going again. I was so fortunate to have these things going for me.

I am so grateful now that I had those privileges. The day came to leave the prison. It's hard to tell you of the excitement that all of us who were leaving were experiencing. But I think back a little bitterly on that naive excitement, now. We were all squealing and laughing and we had all our stuff in bags that our families had sent to us and we were only waiting for the taxis to come and pick us up at the appointed second to take us to our destinations. Of course it was very exciting. Lots of hugs and tears and goodbyes. I was finally taken across the street to be processed out for the last time. I was given the money that was in my account and signed a bunch of paperwork. I received another copy of my social security card. That's it.

A cab came shortly thereafter and drove me away from the prison camp. Now I was excited and once I got to the airport, I bought a coffee and some cigarettes, because I just felt like smoking again. I felt free, but in fact I was on my way to a halfway house with a mandatory stay of six months. Just a different sort of prison, but a prison in its own right. I got on the plane and flew all the way to Newark, New Jersey. Ugly to be here again. I wonder if I have done the right thing. Oh well, it's too late now. I catch a cab and give him the address of the halfway house in the heart of Newark. Oh boy. I knew this would probably stink, but I had no idea how bad. It was never the outside world I had to be reacquainted with; I stepped right up and never blinked in my dealings with "normal" people. It was these changes in institutions and the people living there and the authority figures and rules imposed that would give me the hardest time and the most challenge, as an increasingly spiritual being, to tolerate and not judge, to not overreact and give in to negative emotions. I had eaten yucky food on the plane and was hungry but had no idea at all what to expect from this new place that I was going to have to live at. It was dreadful. Worse than horrible. Worse than prison. This was going to be way tougher than I thought. Strip search and urine test when I announce my arrival at their wonderful establishment. After a long time, and it is already pretty damn late at night, I am taken (with my things still being searched in another room), to my new home. It is a big, long room with bright lights high up there and like eighteen or more beds, nine on each side of the room with just a little locker to keep your stuff in. This is awful. Six months living like this? Maybe I should just violate and go back . . . I am literally thinking like this as I contemplate this newest test. With pure dismay.

I can't tell you how deflated, disillusioned and disappointed and plain devastated I felt after looking forward to this for so long. I saw nowhere to cry, and this was not good. I wanted to curl up into a ball and wail my broken heart out. How I even got through that first night I will never know. I went to take a shower the next morning and was shocked to see that there was just one big stall and four or five shower heads. Any one can just come in and take a shower while you are in here. Not even prison was this bad. I was so unhappy and just had to get in and pray no one came in and of course some one did. Very depressing to think of this being a normal thing. I like to shower every day. I feel so exposed here, worse than prison ever was. And I did forget to mention that there were men sharing this building with us? Oh yeah, randy, scary dudes fresh out of the joint and they were everywhere and very aggressive. I am not an unattractive woman, so I received lots of totally unwanted attention. Just what I needed. The food was a joke and I was starving. There were so many rules: We had to perform some chore every day, whether that was to mop the entire hallway or clean the bathroom or pick up all the cigarette butts outside, after we came home from our regular job. So you worked your butt off all day at work and you came home to this place and had to work some more before you could just take a shower and go to bed. You also had to pay them 25% of your gross paycheck, every paycheck. It was sick. I was going to have to wait until I was working and they had been paid their first tithing until I could leave for the weekends.

That was the good thing though, and the one privilege that made it worth trying to stick out the horrendous living conditions. Once you were working and earning, you could spend the weekend at some place that they would know about (with a phone number where they could reach you). You were not supposed to leave, though, or you had to tell them that, too. Basically, they would know where you would be at every moment that you were away. They could and would call you at this number at any time they liked and you had better be there, or you could get into big trouble and go back to prison. Just like that. When you got to work in the morning, you had to call them. This was after signing out at the moment you walked out the door. If you left work for any reason, you were supposed to call. Right before you left for the halfway house, you called again, and they would record how long it took you to get home. You were not supposed to go anywhere else. It was very intrusive and so regulated and so anal. Confining and suffocating. We were supposedly trying to perform in the real world again and we had to go back to this place daily and be treated like garbage, and having them call every second of the day was ridiculous. It was very difficult at first to remember all of these calls. It was one way that they weeded out the idiots.

I slipped up a few times. I had called Ben over that first traumatic weekend of my arrival. I was still in shock and I was really pathetic on the phone with him. We arranged that he would pick me up at the place on Monday morning and he would take me to work with him. I was feeling like a vulnerable, wounded, tortured puppy, getting kicked from place to place. It's nice for awhile and then WHAM! Something new and having to re-acclimate all over again. It was exhausting and I just wanted this to end. But I was looking at six long months. There had always been something that I had been waiting for. And a new test to pass. Does this ring any bells for anyone? One nice thing over that weekend before I started working was a very young and cute guy I saw, in passing, while I was making sure all my paperwork was right and I could in fact go to work the next day. Everything was a pain in the ass. I wanted to be the hell out of this place and I was going to work. Anyway, this guy saw me when I was in glasses and just out of the shower, in a bathrobe and everything, and he smiled at me and I, startled, definitely smiled back.

Now here was an interesting diversion. I could actually look forward to one thing when I got in at night. Seeing this cutie-pie. He really was a beautiful young man. I had stuff to do that night, but he approached me again soon enough. We began a flirtatious friendship. Going back to work was really wonderful, but there was definitely some weird stuff to deal with that I had not really expected or thought about. I had a secret. Only Ben knew that I was living in a halfway house and that I was fresh out of federal prison; and he absolutely did not want any one else to know about it. He felt it would pre-prejudice people about me and just be generally messy and distracting. He couldn't lose efficiency, you know. It was hard, though, not to want to share with people what I was experiencing in my life, especially after several months when you are very friendly now, and close, yet you still have secrets that might shock people — in fact, probably more so now, because you did not just tell them in the first place.

I am no different than anyone else, for the most part, and I was not and am not ashamed that I went to prison or for what I did beforehand to create that reality for myself. I am the master of my destiny and I believe in my higher nature to do its best to fulfill its destiny. But to me, a secret is a shameful thing and I did not like it that part of my life was to be considered shameful. But he was helping me in every way possible, so I was not going to go against his wishes. I didn't talk about it.

I had got it approved that I could, this very next weekend, go to Ben's apartment for the whole time from Friday night to Sunday night. He had told me that he was going to be spending his weekends at his mom's in Brooklyn and I could stay there, so I could get out of the halfway house. I had no family or friends in NJ and I had nowhere to go. He was so totally generous with his place and his heart and he loaned me money and helped me in numerous ways. But for him, I would have had to spend the weekends at the halfway house, which would have been really depressing. Suicidal. Only the very terrible people did not have a job or people to hang out with on the weekends. You just didn't want to be there. I would tell them that I had to work overtime all the time so I could go back to that hellhole as late as possible every workday.

I was taking cabs to and from work, and once in awhile Bill would take me back and forth. I was trying to get approval to get a car, because this was just ridiculous. It was expensive, and inconvenient, and stupid; yet I had to again fight their stupid little system to get the paperwork and get it approved. Everything was made hard to do with all the red tape involved. You gave them all the information that they required and they just sat on it and did nothing. After many weeks of waiting, we got the stupid approval and I was allowed to drive a nifty old car that Bill had found for $1000. That made a huge difference in the quality of my life there. These are pure freedom issues. Once I had a car to get out of there with, I felt like I was free again, and that this was just an intermission between prison and my real life. Once I could go in the morning and get in a car and drive away, I was just staying there for awhile and I had options. Very empowering and useful tool, a car. This was where my personal freedom transformation took place, simply because I knew that I could do this and it was almost over. I did not loathe the stupid halfway house as much, but doing things like having to go to NA meetings once a week and the stupid chores and the horrible showers . . . Okay, I always detested it. I still could not make any real decisions on my own, obviously. I went to work and came home late and paid them and did their chores and tolerated the arrangements there and waited for the weekends. I was hanging with this cute guy, though, and had taken to picking him up in the morning after I took off in my car. He would already be walking down the road toward the main street and I would stop and get him. We would go drink coffee for a few and make out in the car for another few. He was so young, only about 24, but he was adorable and delicious. We did this for awhile but nothing ever came of it.

I was relying on my inner wisdom and guidance now, as much as I could, and would visualize things happening, manifesting, and putting the energy in motion. Tonianne said she would get in touch with the US Attorney and set it all up and would be in touch in a few days. Oh boy, did I wait like a fiend for that call. Every time the phone rang my heart took a diving leap. She did call, though, and everything was a go. She would be in touch with the miserable halfway house to let them know what I was doing and that paperwork was going to be coming through immediately thereafter to release me forthwith. YAY!! It was early December, 1997. At last, I had been there for three months, the halfway point of my delightful stay in Hotel Hell. For some reason or another, I was once again in touch with Tonianne, my federal attorney from the past. She needed to know if I would be interested in testifying before a grand jury "about Rudy and your/his activities." I asked if there was anything in it for me — what could she perhaps ask them to do for me that was possible? She wondered that, herself, and I just said, look, get me out of the halfway house right after I testify, and I will definitely do it. At least I was smarter and more savvy this time and negotiated something for my efforts. She thought that was reasonable and doable and my heart leaped at the thought. To be free? For real?

The date came to testify. I was nervous and excited, all dressed up for court again. I had been prepared to testify a few other times, and it always fell through, so I was almost looking forward to finally doing this and having that experience under my belt as well. I saw the FBI guy from NJ, William Wilkes, and he looked very surprised to see me there, and said, "Are you already out of prison?" Something charming like that. I never said anything nice about the NJ feds, did I?

I was briefed about what they would be asking me and, since it was only a grand jury, there would be no cross examination, but the people in the grand jury and the judge could also interject questions at some point. That was great. It's not like Rudy would be there and no one would be harassing me from the other side. I went in, and was called, and sat down, ready to answer all of their questions. They were all simple and just dealt with the operation that I had helped Rudy run for a short period of time, so I also answered some questions about myself. I had just been released from prison myself, yes? Yes. This went on for awhile and the judge might ask me to elaborate on some point or what not, but it was very comfortable and non-threatening and I was as specific and detailed as I could be and it was an interesting experience. It was over fairly quickly. I shook a few hands and they thanked me for coming in and testifying and me and Tonianne walked away. She said that the paperwork might take a couple of days, but that I would be getting out by the end of the week, for sure. I was ecstatic and hugged her and thanked her tearfully and profusely. After I left that day, I sent her a bouquet of flowers for her beautiful heart. I also arranged to see some apartments close by work. I had saved up some money and needed a place to move into if this really happened for me. I hated to count on it as a certainty, just in case something happened to delay it. But it sounded like it was really going to happen! I was so hopeful of truly having my freedom, even though I was conveniently forgetting that I still had three years of supervised release that would begin as soon as I was out of the halfway house. But I always just crossed those new bridges when I came to them, as you have seen from this account.

On December 18th, 1997, I was released from the halfway house, two days (I think) after testifying for the grand jury in Newark, NJ. It was exactly two years from the date of my surrendering to the prison camp in Phoenix. It was a simply stunning and marvelous feeling to be in that case manager's office at the halfway house, signing papers with my bags packed up beside me, in the middle of the day. I was so ready to leave. They seemed very surprised that this had actually happened and that made it all the more fun for me to see their expressions as I did the processing-out thing and got ready to take my leave of their controlling company. Within minutes, I drove away from that contaminated, dark place and never looked back.

I had gotten my new apartment, and it was partially furnished, so there was a bed that I was going to sleep on in a place that was all mine! I was overjoyed to be experiencing this beautiful rush of freedom earlier than I had dreamed possible and, oh, the feelings of gratitude to the Divine One who had been continuously looking out for me throughout this time, for my whole life. This just put me into a beautiful space and peace of mind and confidence and dreams of the future and all the possibilities if one only saw them and made efforts to make them come true. When I slept alone that night, after taking the most blissful and solitary shower that I have ever experienced, I was blissed out completely. So happy that your heart feels close to bursting in pure gratitude and happiness.

I had to get in touch with both the federal probation officer and a state parole officer the next day. I was going to be on both parole and probation. Yippee! It was still one of the most wonderful mornings of my life. My own bathroom! My own shower!! No other people!! It's very hard to describe how precious being alone is after living in prison, where you can never really be all alone. It is one of the most common things that is to be cherished and is usually taken for granted. Even the military is close, but lots of people choose that career.

Most people don't think they choose to go to prison, yet they do. I did. I tried to get out of it, but I created this in my life and I was going to go to prison because I chose to. All of us humans must stand up, get real, and take responsibility for our actions, decisions, choices. Too many people have someone ready to blame for everything that has gone wrong. It's always somebody else's fault. Our Life is our own Creation. I made choices. I made decisions. I take responsibility for all of my choices and decisions. All of my actions. No more hiding and blaming. Everything I have ever done has been of my choosing and there is no one to blame. Everything I have done has made me who I am today, and I am proud of who I am and I regret none of my choices. I accept it all and move forward with living my Life. Everything is a lesson. Everything is a blessing. Life is rich and beautiful and abundant and filled with love if you choose to be aware of it, swirling all around us.

Getting ready for work for the first time in my new apartment was a joyous experience. I was grateful for every little thing. There was nothing that could wipe the huge grin off my face. It felt so good to be back on my own.

I just was not prepared for the supervised release being so tough. I had no idea (once again) what this would be like. I made appointments with both offices for the following days. For today, I was blissfully free and unaware of what next awaited me. The federal probation officer was a very nice guy and I felt blessed that I could be dealing with him and not another one that would not be this decent. I shouldn't have jinxed myself. We talked about my past and arrangements to pay off my fine, which I had been forced to start paying in little increments, even in prison. I had to have the entire amount paid off by the end of the three-year period that I was to be supervised by them. I had to give them a urine sample and he said that he would be in touch about the next time we needed to get together. He said he would need to see my house, so he would be stopping by at some point soon. The test was done in front of me, and it was of course negative. I had not had any weed or anything else since that cocaine in Arizona. I was totally clean and so I did not mind at all peeing in a cup for them.

The parole officer was also a pretty cool guy and it was the same deal; need a urine sample, need to see where you live, need you to start paying your fine. This seemed like it was going to be no big deal. I slipped right back into living alone and being "out" like I was Miss Adaptability. I didn't miss a beat. I was taking on lots more responsibilities at work and it was fun to go to the market again and take care of all the little things. I was loving life on every level possible. I was taking nothing at all for granted and everything looked shiny and new and stunning. I had not a complaint in the world. Everyone should go to prison for a year and come out feeling like I felt. It would change the world. Imagine not just taking things for granted, like bathing alone, or having a light on or off. And not appreciating every single blessed second of Life, and the freedoms that we all do indeed take for granted.

This new perspective and grateful attitude and awareness of love in everything does not last forever, but it is there with you for as long as you nurture it and embrace it and it can last a long time. It's a beautiful thing to experience and I am really honored that I was allowed to be made aware of so much about living and love. I shined this enthusiasm outwards and people responded very positively for the most part. This is what it's like to be aware that we have Light within and consciously turning it on!

The parole situation went on very easily for almost the whole time I had to do it, but unfortunately for me the probation guy handed me over to a woman who was supposedly the "drug" P.O. officer and because of my past history with drugs and the fact that I had completed the 500-hour drug program in prison, I was stuck with her for awhile. She was a total control freak. Very scary woman. I detested her instantly. Interacting with her was awful and we got off to a bad start and never recovered from there. She could see and feel my dislike, as I was not going to hide my disdain for her. I was not out and out rude, but I was as unresponsive as I could be and I just wanted to get out of her presence. She wanted to ask questions and tell me what this time of supervised release would be like. For the first thing, she was going to force me to go some place once a week and see this man, a drug counselor or something. I was adamantly opposed. I have a very important job, I said, and I don't have time for this unnecessary stuff. I just completed a 500-hour drug program, for Christ's sake! There are no drugs in my urine. Why do I have to do such a stupid thing — drive to Newark to see you every other week, again to see him once a week, and over to this far off town to see the parole officer. All this, just weeks after getting out of a halfway house that had gone out of its way (not all of them do) to make life miserable for everyone who is forced to live there.

After all of this, it just seems to me that the system is screwed up and blinded by its own massiveness. I had done everything right up to this point, during all the torment that I had gone through, and this was how I was treated upon release? This was supposed to support and encourage me to continue to do the right thing? Everything that most of them had thrown at me seemed only geared to frustrate me enough to go off and do something stupid that would get me in trouble so they could think that they had "broken" me. I felt that since they had never broken me yet, they were on some level still trying to get under my skin, so they could point and shriek, "AHA!" and tell me I was dirt and would always be dirt . . . prison stuff, trying to demolish your self-esteem and make you feel utterly submissive. I had been very good in prison, but for my own reasons, reasons that this woman was never going to grasp or understand. Another blessed test. Okay.

I argued about it, but she was going to have her way and what could I really say? I was furious however, and left there in the worst mood I had felt since the lovely halfway house days. I saw the guy for the first time soon after and he acted like he was some psychiatrist and asked me probing questions and studied my face, saying nothing; and I just thought I might go berserk and let them win after all. It was just one thing after another, it seemed, and I did not want to lose this beautiful feeling of gratitude and love and peace and this was pushing me too far. It was just too much nonsense that had no purpose; I was being treated as if I had just got out of rehab and not prison for two years. I could understand this treatment if I had been using in prison and/or after, in the halfway house, or something. But to be drug-free for years and have to undergo these ridiculous exercises they were making me endure?

I was very upset and stressed out. This was no way to help me get reacquainted with being "free" or anything of the sort. They were making life harder than was ever necessary.

Why this is allowed to happen? I somehow got through living like this for months, but their little demands made me long for a joint. Having to go to this drug guy made me want to get high more than any other single experience that I had had in or out of prison. It was ludicrous. It was all I could do to try to be civil, same as with that ghastly probation officer. But I was going, and scoring points, even though I had virtually nothing to say to this mostly well-intentioned man. I had worked these things out on my own. I had attended and actively participated in a year-long drug program that had taught me a lot and I was practicing the tools I had learned as well as I could. There was nothing to say!

Even when I had been doing a lot of drugs, I had never been addicted to any of them, no matter how much or often I did them. I could take 'em or leave 'em. I usually did take them, but I functioned in my life at all times. It was never an issue. Even that,.this dude could not get through his head. It was a complete waste of time and you all know how I feel about having to say that. How depressing. Finally, after many, many months, it was over and I did not have to go see him anymore. Sooner or later I lost the horrid woman P.O. as well.

It was all still so controlling over my entire life. If, for instance, you wanted to visit your mom in Colorado, you had to get approval and permission and let them know everything that you would be doing, going, staying. Invasive and untrusting, every step of the way. So even though I was technically "free," it was an illusion. I couldn't get a passport (which is fine), or own a firearm. Never had one; why would I buy one now?

Was the system set up to assist and encourage and support newly freed convicts? Or to hamper them with having to jump through these hoops? Everything in the big, blind system is so generalized and there is nothing happening on the individual level. It's a shame. How was that conducive to my continuing exemplary behavior, which was all I, personally, had ever shown? There are a lot of cracks in this sidewalk, unfortunately.

I chose this experience, though, and once again I struggled with trying to find the blessing here and what I should be learning. I have found and lost love, and will most likely do so again, but I am learning and growing and experiencing life.

Finally, on December 17th, 2000, I was finished with the probation, three years of supervised release that had never eased up until the very end. Now I am Free . . . To live my Life any way I see fit. To fulfill my Destiny and purpose. To spread Light instead of shadows. To do the best at all things I endeavor to do. My faith and trust in All That Is is strong and my own personal power and strength is at its height, and expanding, very much due to all that I have experienced and felt compelled to do in my fairly short life. My purpose is truly to help others through my story of growth and change. I am only hoping that something in my story helps someone to keep going in a difficult situation, or to explore their spirituality, or whatever chords this may strike within one's soul. Hetep to all.

Linda's Profile — And Her Integration Back Into Society

Linda is clear that at a pivotal moment in her life she changed direction from over-achiever to under-achiever. Her trust in her father's affection was destroyed when she bore the brunt of his disappointment, his humiliation. Time would create an evolution within her identity — a sense of self-loathing as well as a simultaneous hatred for the pressures put on her. She found refuge in those who understood her rage; they wore it in their clothing, they played it on their thrashing guitars, they attempted to numb it with their drugs. They searched to find love in sex with like-minded dysfunctional lost souls.

It began to make sense that a man might finally come to her rescue, evoking emotions that a father or male caretaker represents: order, authority, and love. If Linda could satisfy all these criteria, she had finally succeeded. For such an aphrodisiac, she would find herself willing to sacrifice anything.

Whatever self-esteem Linda might have maintained, she was stripped of it during her prison experience. "Sensory deprivation" is another way of saying she felt unable to "cope with the multitude of realities that prison forces you to forget; by submission or by force, (you) learn to follow a format. It doesn't include re-learning how to exist within society; no matter if release date is inevitable."

Back into Community Life: A City Proves Restorative Justice is Alive and Well

It has taken many years for Linda to understand why she committed her crimes, but during those years she also became the kind of person who might be able to see that truth. She is finally living and functioning within her community. She "keeps secrets, feels at times like she is forced to be dual and that even while she makes friends, she figures they'll abandon her if the 'truth' be known . . . it's unhealthy . . . time will help me learn not to feel shame. But I've had to do that work on my own: those steps from admittance to fear of punishment to acceptance and self-love. I do deserve it. I committed a felony; it was wrong, but there will always be the layers that led me to that point, and figuring those out, I feel I can stop hating. I feel I can breathe, and deserve that . . . ."

Sometimes a city has proven itself capable of supporting the processes a victim experiences, as well as the offender. Sometimes, pilot communities show they have worked restorative justice in such a way that most residents would prefer this more liberal and gracious theory to a sense of fear or hatred toward the "ex-con."

Batavia, New York is a small town just thirty miles outside Buffalo, a community that rests within the Genesee County. To look at the small, historical town with its craftsman homes and tree-lined streets, children walking in groups to school . . . it seems almost to be in a time warp. In truth, its one of our countries models for the future.

New York State has the fastest growing prison population. You wouldn't guess that, either, if you judged by Batavia. As sublime as its beauty, so serene is the personality. An entire community is to be thanked for this; each member involved in his own way: from how the gas station attendant attends meetings on how to deal with "the guy they read about in the papers . . ." to the victims' groups and the county defenders. But in the early 1980s, the time when restorative justice was taken from a thought to a working process, the courage and the vision came from former Genesee County Sheriff Douglas Call.

With yet another prison under development only a short distance from his house, Sheriff Call did not feel that released offenders deserved to "restore," but rather they should have to work off their punishment. It wasn't enough to serve jail time; it was more appropriate to come back into a town and give the community what it deserved: some hard work from someone who'd been willing to take responsibility for the damage he'd caused. The success, and the harmony of the program, would dawn on him in the months to come. For the time being, the good sheriff was thinking in terms of his own concept of "just deserts." So, with the help of veteran probation officer Dennis Wittman, a plan to develop a program for sentencing offenders to community service and including victims in the criminal justice process was created.[18] Wittman was all for the idea: "When I was in probation, I saw a system that was very one-sided." He described how it dealt with offenders only, forcing Wittman to constantly ask himself "What about the victims? Where are they?"

And of course, there was the cost. Genesee County Manager Jay Gsell wrote, "From a county government perspective, it's big money in terms of the cost of the whole criminal justice system. And then certain parts of it are more expensive than others, if we just take the attitude that anybody who does something wrong needs to spend time in a facility." Another voice was agreeing, and coming together to support new ideals. Ironically, a town only ten miles from Attica (the infamous prison) was joining on the next level as news spread. There were leaders in this community who realized that traditional imprisonment wasn't working; political leaders may have loved it, but there was really no evidence to prohibit this group of people from trying a new process. One contributor

18.Crime, Shame and Re-Integration, 1989, John Braithwaite, Cambridge University Press.

notes, "[The traditional approach] is real convenient because it says you're being tough on crime. It's actually short-sighted: it oversimplifies how to deal with the problems. Not the least of which is the staggering number of prisoners who recidivate — up to two-thirds in many states."[19]

With enough people in a position to actually make the prospect of restorative justice work, the community now had to act. Of course, that's the hard part. It requires both (a) identifiably remorseful persons, convincing enough to earn acceptance back in the community, and (b) a variety of mechanisms — community service, meetings between the offenders and their victims, and the pre-sentencing "diversion" — that allows offenders to earn back their place in the community. This would be an experiment with the offenders, but equally or more so, with the tolerance of the community.

Jonathon and Steve were two teens who burglarized their school after a night of partying. Thousands upon thousands of dollars' worth of equipment was either ruined or stolen. The boys were sentenced to felony charges. Other boys who were also involved were taken into custody immediately — and Jonathon and Steve went to see Wittman.

A plan was made; after several discussions with family members of the offenders, working a "deal" with a cooperative judge, and with both defense and prosecutors also willing, the boys were given work assignments and several conditions to follow. If they adhered to this plan, Genesee Justice's pre-sentence diversion track, they would stay out of the (juvenile) detention facility and might even clear their records.[20]

Jonathon was assigned community service at a religious retreat center and Steve went to work at a nursing home. With the income they earned, they first had to pay back all the damages they were responsible for. They also had to abide by a curfew and random checks — from police

19. Internet Edition, "Nation's Center For Intervention," 1999, Sara Dyskovsky.
20. *When A Child Goes To Prison*, Christian Book Publications, 1983, Charles Riley.

to probation officers; their lives were very much in the hands of the community. It was also expected, as part of this restorative justice modular, that each boy write an essay about respecting another person's property.

"The worst part was probably going before my classmates, which was part of the deal, and reading that paper," recalls Jonathon. "I have to say, I expected boo's and all that, but the kids and the teachers . . . everyone, basically, seemed thankful, not mad. It was so cool. I had done this horrible thing, and yet, here I was, being welcomed back by everyone; it's just — inside, I knew I needed to keep up the momentum. But it was not so scary, not with all that support." His co-conspirator in crime adds that the nursing home checks "(inspired me) to get another job, too. I liked the money. I liked the respect of earning it. I didn't have to avoid people, I could look at them . . ."

Both agree that the curfew was rough, but in retrospect, being home instead of running amok on the streets forced them to spend time with their families. "We're closer now, which keeps me more connected to the program. I don't want to disappoint these people, and I don't want to disappoint my parents. God, I think of where I was heading, now that I see more clearly. I can see how it happens, like a snowball . . . pretty soon it's felony and penitentiaries or murder or something — all for money or whatever instant gratification . . . that's not nearly as positive as the respect," considers Jonathon.

Wittman knows exactly what Jonathon is talking about: heading off the creation of another habitual criminal. Without knowing it, "Jonathon was on his way . . ."

But Wittman wants it made clear that restorative justice isn't specifically oriented to youths. His office handles many far more serious crimes and criminals. In response, Genesee Justice has negotiated "split" sentences — community sentencing plus jail time — in manslaughter, assault, domestic violence and sexual assault cases. Offenders are compelled to make restitution, pay for victims' counseling and perform community service in addition to serving time in incarceration. Early on, Genesee Justice even participated in the case of a sniper.[21]

The Role of Faith in Restorative Justice

Chuck Colson pioneered what is now the worldwide organization, Prison Fellowship Ministries, as mentioned above. With the participation of innumerable Christian volunteers, PF brings its positive philosophy to places as dark as the Angola prison that inspired the movie, *Dead Man Walking.* Of course, the Restorative Justice methodology is not tied only to one religion, and is available to be adapted and implemented as appropriate within different cultures.

Spirituality and politics are usually separated. However, Genesee County's program is working, and hasn't as yet faced any legal challenge regarding its integration of policy and prayer. Public defender Gary Horton offers that his clients maintain a wide variety of spiritual beliefs. It isn't his job, he explains, to favor one or another, but to encourage any religion that provides solace. "Systematically, we try to reach out to churches and because they are made up of basically kind persons, and are predisposed to those things we're trying to achieve, we condone any aid from any spiritual group . . ."

Wittman is adamant that the program is successful largely due to its emphasis on the promotion of a strong Judeo-Christian approach to justice. "With victims and with offenders, we've actively involved the church. That faith base can sustain people through some difficult times. Our entire staff carries that spirituality about them." And faith filters throughout the community; not synods or specific belief systems, but the ideology that there must be a reliance on spirit. An example is illustrated when a fifteen-year-old male was shot to death by a close acquaintance,

21. Internet Edition, "Capitol Punishment and Restorative Justice," 2001, Chuck Colson.

also a juvenile. Several churches worked together to facilitate the healing process for the families involved. From a planned meeting between families to a prayer vigil, the community gathered round to aid, to offer collective healing.

What makes restorative justice work in Batavia has everything to do with the power of great minds working together, as harmoniously as a criminal situation might allow. It has everything to do with agency effort, community service and treatment, sentencing plans, and ultimately, acceptance — at life's most un-accepting times. "It's become obvious that the public defenders aren't here to get bad guys good deals. We don't want to see victims unprotected, nor do we promote the over-housing of prisons. Collectively, we encourage programs that give clients an opportunity, presuming they have offended; to break the cycle they're in and avoid re-offending in the future. And that's where we can establish some real common ground on alternatives and 'rest.-rive'-type programs."

For at least two decades the United Nations has taken notice of restorative justice, mediation and informal means of working with specific crimes and criminals. Intergovernmental documents that relate to restorative justice, from both the United Nations and the Council of Europe, include:

- The Declaration of Basic Principles of Justice for Victims of Crime and Abuse of Power (1985)
- Standard Minimum Rules for the Administration of Juvenile Justice (Beijing Ruling, 1985 — General Assembly)
- Victims of Crime and Abuse of Power, 1990 Economic and Social Council
- Basic Principles on the Use of Force and Firearms by Law Enforcement Officials, 1990 — Eight United Nations Congress on the Preventions of Crime and the Treatment of Offenders
- Standard Minimum Rules for Non-Custodial measures (Tokyo) 1990 — General Assembly

These regulations or policies refer to restorative justice, or at the very least, to restorative processes such as mediation.

As a further important sign that restorative justice has been recognized as being effective, these standards were employed after the acts of terrorism were perpetrated on September 11, 2001 in New York, Pennsylvania and Washington. A wide range of organizations and individuals (Victim Offender Mediation, Forgiveness in International Responses, volunteered service from trauma and crisis specialists, clergy, the Children as Victims and Perpetrators of Crime, and the United Nations Criminal Justice Program, Guidelines for Technical Assistance in the Field of Urban Crime Prevention) and a wide range of methods and approaches, inspired by the roots of restorative justice policy, were brought to bear.[22]

In 1999, ECOSOC (the UN Economic and Social Council) enforced a ruling, which called for an escalated use of mediation and restorative justice, and suggested that the UN Commission on Crime Prevention and Criminal Justice consider developing standards to guide nations in using these forms of intervention. This set some guidelines, but each of the 37 countries who have adopted restorative justice policy has also implemented its own variation, adhering to basic standards of restorative justice with adaptations to accommodate local culture and a variety of social issues.

In fact, criminal justice experts from every region met in Ottawa from October 29 to November 1, 2001 to discuss the proposed Basic Principles on the Use of Restorative Justice Programs in Criminal Matters. The purpose was to review comments by each of the 37 countries on draft versions of the basic principles, as circulated by the Secretary-General in late 2000.[23]

The Alliance of National Guidelines of Offenders on Crime Prevention and the Treatment of Offenders has been preparing updated formats. Utilizing the Council of Europe provisions as well as standards

---

22. "A Chance to Give Back Peace," *Lexington Herald-Leader*, September 15, 1999, Linda Harvey.

23. *Justice in Global Effort*, Sentencing Alternatives, Purich Publishing, 1998, Ross Green.

prepared by other NGOs, the Alliance's Working Party on Restorative Justice completed a draft set of Basic Principles on the Use of Restorative Justice Programs in Criminal Matters in late 1999. These were circulated to countries in anticipation of the Tenth UN Congress on the Prevention of Crime and the Treatment of Offenders (not to be confused with the mistreatment of victims), held in Vienna in April 2000.

At the Congress, forty nations sponsored a resolution providing for distribution of the draft Basic Principles for comment. This resolution was adopted by the Commission and then by ECOSOC. The meeting garnered such favorable response that the Secretary-General was sparked to distribute a letter to all Member States of the United Nations, as well as to Non-Governmental Organizations, asking whether an international instrument on restorative justice would be useful, whether there were substantive comments on the daft, and whether an expert meeting on the topic would be useful. According to the UN Center for International Crime Prevention, it was due to this documentation, in large part, that almost all forty countries submitted the requested responses. This was seven more than the number required by the United Nations before taking further action. Next, an Expert Meeting, a committee made up of leaders and stakeholders within the restorative justice programs worldwide will meet in Canada to refine the latest module.[24]

Restorative justice has been elevated to a global policy by a pool of passionate believers in a system based on the concept of grace, rather than retribution. Unique and visionary individuals within each community help ignite that passion. They make educating themselves on policy a personal mission. Dr. Mario Ottoboni, a Brazilian lawyer, is one such man.

Dr. Ottoboni became concerned about all the people imprisoned of his own city — and the unfair conditions, including starvation and filth and lack of defense. He was inspired to seek a better approach to the

---

24. "Prevention of Crime, Treatment of Offenders," Speech (audio), 2000, Delegate April to 10th UN Congress, Marc Forget.

problem. The doctor joined hands with a group of dedicated church laymen, including Dr. Silvio Marques, a magistrate, and Dr. Hugo Veronese, an educational psychologist, and formed the Association for Protection and Assistance to the Convicted. Together, they developed what is now referred to as the APAC methodology. It was applied in Humaita Prison, in San Jose do Camps, Sao Paulo, Brazil.[25]

Over the last 25 years, APAC has gained international recognition as an effective approach to reducing recidivism rates (re-incarceration). Several fellowships are utilizing this prison regimen under a change in prison management style.

The APAC methodology[26] is structured on five basic principles, which may be interpreted differently depending on cultural and religions traditions:

Unconditional love permeates the atmosphere the prison. This is based upon God's love, a sacrificial love for each individual.

Human Valorization helps the person to become fully aware of his or her innate human dignity and empowered to develop all of his or her capabilities.

Evangelization includes ministering to physical needs and other needs such as medical care, legal aid, social work, and employment assistance as well as sharing the Gospel.

Spiritual Transformation provides a participant every opportunity to take the journey from spiritual crisis to renewal.

---

25. Max Lucado, 2002. Internet Edition, "A Prison Ideal(ology)," date not provided; and Max Lucado, 2002. "Christian Prison," in Praise for Thee [online]. Available at ‹http://www.praise4thee.com/christian_prison.htm›.

26. Lynette Parker, 2002. "Growing Interest in Innovative Prison Management System." In Restorative Justice.org [online], a service of the International Centre for Justice and Reconciliation. Washington, DC: Prison Fellowship International. November 2001 [cited 8 August 2002]. Available from World Wide Web: ‹http://www.restorativejustice.org/rj3/Feature/APAC.htm›.

Reintegration and restoration address the need to restore and strengthen family relationships, and to integrate prisoners positively into society with the help of godparents, mentors, and other PF volunteers.

The structure's impact has been strong within the community environment as well as among prisoners, volunteers, and those who foster spiritual, behavioral and lifestyle changes.

In 1989, APAC became the Brazilian affiliate of Prison Fellowship International (PF). In the 1990s, the methodology was adopted by PF in Ecuador, Peru, Argentina and the United States. And because of the interest, the PF International conducted a research project between 1998 and 2000 to identify a strategy for adapting the format in other cultures and countries while maintaining its integrity.

While we will scrutinize specific measurements of restorative justice, both the pro's and the con's, the methodology and effectiveness of APAC holds a unique place within the categorization of clinical modelers, in that is examines the emotional and spiritual bases of the program, as well as the clinical positives and negatives.

Spiritual input has a positive effect in this process, as Linda's autobiographical sketch acknowledges. This has also been documented in research studies. In 1997, a study showed that inmates who participated in Prison Fellowship Bible studies ten times a year, in four New York State prisons, appeared to have less tendency toward recidivism. In Brazil, Johnson compared recidivism of the APAC-based Humaita prison with an innovative model prison at Branganca. Both models produced dramatically lower rates of recidivism (the general average was 50-75%), but Humaita — whose inmates were considered to be at a higher risk for re-offending, since they were convicted of more violent crimes — came in at just 16%, whereas a rate of 36% was reported for Branganca.

In South Africa, the Center for Restorative Justice has become instrumental in bringing a new calm to a notoriously conflicted region.[27] The Center provides information, services and research to further the development of restorative justice, founded in 1988. Just two social workers began the foundation, exposing the principles through a family group conferencing pilot project sponsored by their Inter-Ministerial Committee on Young People at Risk. Again, we see the positive impact of the individual on the community at large.

The Center's vision was to undertake similar projects to significantly change the crime situation in South Africa. The conclusion so far are indicative of the RJC's commitment to research, education, training, sourcing funding for other restorative justice organizations, advocacy of the RJ paradigm and a number of projects at home in South Africa.

As in Batavia (New York) or Brazil, a specific adaptation of restorative justice policies was employed, to meet the particulars of South Africa. Policy makers attempt to provide for the region while simultaneously creating global strategies.[28] The focus is a combination of current, completed and future research and training projects conducted by the Center for Restorative Justice in South Africa. Some of those include:

A. Helping the Khayalami Metropolitan Council develop a restorative approach to abuse management.

B. Holding a Restorative Justice Day workshop for the senior management of the Department of Correction Services

C. Providing services in developing a drama therapy diversion program and victim offender conference

D. Developing a library containing restorative justice materials and research.

---

27. South Africa: The Real Threat to Sustainable Democracy (Commentary 44), Duncan Edmunds, Canadian Security Intelligence, May 1994
28. Internet Edition, "Intergovermental and Global Impacts of Restorative Justice," January, 1997.

E. A web site featuring g resources, research reports, and charity events for the National Organization for Victim Assistance.

F. Information regarding terrorism response, assembled by the National Center for Victims of Crime.

Chuck Colson describes how prison fellowship and restorative justice programs and principles work not only together internationally, but also within political boundaries.

The PF program came about when a hard-headed warden refused to release inmates for our Washington discipleship program. 'Bring your program inside the prison,' he insisted. We did — and today seminars are held in 1,200 prisons every year. It seemed we were merely responding to needs or opportunities of the here and now: in hindsight, a clear sense of divine providence emerges. We now see that there is a spiritual thread; most important, our vision is not limited, but a worldview — I describe in a previous book that spirit is about more than personal salvation — it is a way of understanding reality. It answers the fundamental questions raised from the beginning of time: Where did we come from? Why is there evil and suffering? How can it be fixed?

Colson's questions are not limited to the U.S. These issues are global — and restorative justice demands recognition of this. Law is not solely based on the judgment of a man in a cloak banging a gavel; so when "justice" is seeking legal reform, its goal is to reflect transcendent standards, the very foundation of restorative justice.

Evil. The dominant view is that some people are innately evil, and deserve punishment. Restorative belief says that, just as a person can be restored, he must at one point have been *good*, to create this possibility. That, in fact, "evil" may be about circumstance, and the choices made accordingly. Humans are basically good. Crime is caused by unjust social structures — most often, oppression, poverty, and abuse. Political liberals insist that crime can be cured through rehabilitation. Conservatives favor harsh sentences to deter crime — but we now recognize this approach to be futile. Where is the middle ground? If we accept that a criminal was not always criminal, but recognize that once a crime has been committed a penalty must be enforced — how harsh, or inhumane, or how "soft" should it be?

Rejecting the utopianism of either/or theories, crime can be defined, according to restorative justice, as a moral choice — no matter what the mitigating circumstance. One must accept accountability; but that des not mean that one must be ostracized or labeled *innately* monstrous, as if he (or she) had no choice, was beyond hope to begin with and will always be hopeless.

Establishing that crime may stem mostly from "choice," the third issue, then, is repentance, and the restoration of peace and harmony for the offender and the community. To be specific, in-prison seminars and the encouraging of marriage and family in spite of lockdown facilities plays a role in healing. Like a community that must learn to allow the offender back into its domain, the family, too, should attempt to accept a repentant offender. Below, we will present some statistics that indicate the importance of family to the prisoner.

Mentoring programs also help inmates re-integrate into their communities. For example, Detroit's TOP program (Transition of Prisoners) which has reduced recidivism among its participants to six percent in one of the toughest areas of America.[29]

---

29. Rhapsodies of a Repeat Offender, Persea Books, 1995, Wayne Koesttenbum.

When the National Institute of Mental Health studied high-risk inner-city neighborhoods, they found that just 6% of children from stable, safe families became delinquent, but 90% of children from unstable, (mostly) one-parent families who lacked parental supervision and regular, sufficient income, did.[30] And while poverty and race are issues that need to be studied in relation to crime, this chapter takes a broader look at the family unit, and at the lack of moral training many criminals experienced during their formative years, regardless of most other factors. As Dr. John Forsythe said, "Take away the family, and we might as well build [prison] cells right now."

It's difficult enough for a child to feel stable if his or her family unit is dysfunctional (argumentative, abusive, etc.). A major step is taken further in the wrong direction, when one parent lands behind bars. The number one indicator of criminal behavior is having a parent locked up — one study found 84% of boys who become serious juvenile offenders have a parent or sibling in jail.[31] Imagine,

---

30. Washington, DC. National Institute of Mental Health, National Institute of Mental Health Publications, 1968, John Gachs.

31. *When A Parent Goes To Jail: A Comprehensive Guide For Counseling Children of Incarcerated Parents*, Rayve Publications, 2000, Rebecca Yaffe.

without intervention, generation upon generation continuing to send family members to prison. Serial killer Gerald Gallego (accused of rape, torture and murder in three states, and sentenced to die at San Quentin in California) wrote:

> My mother never wanted anyone to know about my father. They executed him. He was a pervert. Sometimes, I wonder if my own perversions were genetic, or somehow just picked up by what little I did see of him before he was taken away; or was I just pissed, or did I think maybe it was predestined? Whatever, just like my old man, I'm on death row . . . waiting . . . maybe he'll have some answers.

Even President Bush acknowledged, during his Inaugural Address in 2000, "The proliferation of prisons, however necessary, is no substitute for hope and order in our souls." So what is the solution? How do we bring families together when one member sits locked behind bars? Statistics show that family works as an incentive for restoration among inmates. Even the government agrees, and recently repealed easy divorce laws for inmates, to illustrate the emphasis on family life.

Family and crime: the correlation seems odd. Still, whether we support or decry restorative justice, the strong influence of family on a person's future must be embraced and utilized, in society's self-interest. It should be clear that the steady assault of dysfunctional relationships, left unattended, will continue to unleash chaos on all levels — nationally and internationally.

Case Study: The Johnsons

Laura and Nick were married five years when Nick was sentenced to serve five years at Corsica in California. Nick felt "from the first days I was gone that Laura was shifting . . . moving away from me. I had done a crime. I had to be away, but I didn't want to lose Laura. I went to work, trying to find resolve."

Nick wrote out a list of his own issues, citing problems from his end of the marriage that might be creating its dissolution — it wasn't just about the prison.

> "I was self-pitying, I realized I hadn't even told her I was sorry for my actions, so caught up in my punishment, not even considering she was being punished, too. Saying this to her seemed to build trust. And from there, she seemed to slowly warm to me again. Finally, she said the words, 'I forgive,' and I knew there was hope. Now, during visitations I keep aware of our discussions. I make sure I don't ramble on about my dismal life. I know she knows. It's not necessary to ruin each visit with the obvious. I'm encouraged to work on my issues — my criminal behavior. I want to be sure I'll be free forever, to care for her, to care for myself . . . "

Laura responded to her husband's perspective.

> "Today, I feel confidant we'll get through this. But when he felt nothing, showed nothing but sorrow for the self, I couldn't see a man who felt sorrow about his actions. That was frightening. I thought, 'how could a man commit a crime that lands him in federal prison and think only of himself?' I was moving very far from the marriage, internally — and then, Nick decided he had a role in his actions. Now we work to identify the 'why' and how to prohibit this in the future. Thus, we now have a future . . . ."

Whether or not people take issue with mitigating circumstances, statically we see that families that are broken, either through divorce or simply dysfunction, are likely to rear children who mirror the images within their environments. And some will act out. Rage is an emotion much different than anger. Like sadness is to depression, so is anger to rage. Sadness is identified on the spot: saying good-bye to a lost lover, or a dying pet. Depression is the repressed sense of hopelessness over a long period of time. Anger is similar to sadness in so far that it is momentary. A fight at school or with a parent or spouse. Terrifyingly, rage is an emotion born of the inability to express emotion. And who could express the feelings that are stirred by observing arguments, drinking, drugging and much worse, sexual violations and/or kidnap by an estranged parent? If feelings of fear and anger are not recognized and addressed, rage will evolve. Rage encompasses something powerful, something greater than actual events at hand, so that there is an over-reaction to circumstance. This over-reaction is one facto that leads to criminal behavior, and ultimately to prison. When we understand this human tendency, intervention is possible — so long as social funding and the will are maintained. So long as at least one family member is willing to speak up, and participate. Often, dysfunctional families remain silent, keeping family secrets, perpetuating problems. In the end, the prison population will drop and the need for building projects will diminish tremendously, if society takes the time, and makes the effort to identify that child who has surpassed anger, engulfing rather a sense of rage, and intervenes to make repairs to this precious life before it is turned toward criminal conduct.

The emphasis on harmony within the home is one of the most powerful tools a culture has. How one achieves for her/his children a sense of peace and freedom from fear is not so important, so long as it is in fact, achieved. The overall effect is clear.

CHILDREN AND RESTORATIVE JUSTICE

Nowhere is the need for team support more evident than when crimes are committed against children. When a child is abused, the damage doesn't end when the crime is reported. Suddenly, people in uniforms are asking questions. People in white coats are asking questions. Mommy's crying. And the child has to keep talking about the unspeakable, telling all these people what happened. And remembering how much it hurt.

We have to find a way to respond to such abuses without adding to the trauma caused to children by the very system that was intended to protect them.[32]

A coordinator who works with children and trauma emphasizes the need for a holistic approach to crime: reaching out to both victims and offenders, to repair the harm that's been done. "It keeps you balanced," the coordinator offers. "I used to think I could never work with offenders. It used to tear me up, the guilt of helping a violator. But now, I see it's a part of the equation that must be considered and also . . . healed."[33]

---

32. When Andy's Father Went to Prison, Whitman and Co., 1999, Larry Raymond and Albert Whitman.

33.Internet Edition, Risk Assessment Management, Colorado Department of Justice Resource.

Case Study

> We were a family that didn't have tragedies [says Eve Dillon]. Many
> times a child is killed, a mother dies early, or a father dies early. We
> had parents ourselves that had lived to be in their nineties, and we
> had often commented that most people had terrible tragedies —
> children were rushed to the hospital with broken backs or
> something — and we just didn't have things like that happen in our
> lives.

All that changed on September 23, 1983 when Eve's husband was
murdered. "Normalcy" vanished.

Less than a month after the murder, Eve was contacted by her
community's victim-assistance program with offers to help.

> It was the greatest thing that ever happened to me. I never would
> have gotten though this tragedy. These people went to court with
> me, they explained everything. It was two years before my
> husband's case went to court and in that period, I was never alone.

Eve was so impressed with the victim-assistance program that she
ultimately became a volunteer.

> This ability to work with a victim and an offender at the same time
> is phenomenal. I know many people couldn't do it, but those who
> can are those making a societal change. My children were able to
> cope without hating, without raging. Does the world at large
> understand what that meant to their future(s)?

Not enabling offenders to continue to harm children is a huge issue.
That is one argument against restorative justice: If a man (or woman) has
molested or murdered a child, how can this person, at this level of
deviancy, be approached through a methodology based on conflict

resolution? But one community after another is convinced that the answer is at hand: Everyone can experience change through restorative justice.

> It's time consuming [explains Eve], "but if you ask people how they feel about their own city's justice system, the response is mostly negative. So, better some long hours than no results. We're never going to replace our dysfunctional justice system. Our children are just as victimized by that as anything; but there are other ways to look at crime than just punishment — to show our children that with the investment of time and emotion, meaningful change occurs. We worry about our children's safety — we must take into consideration their minds. Society is constantly screaming about television programming — what about a failed judicial system? What might frighten a child more: a cartoon monster or a daddy forgotten on his parole date because his papers got lost? Which message is least hopeful, really?

The best response to such questions comes from an imprisoned father, David Moore.

His sixteen-year-old son David III lives in the Intensive Treatment Unit in near Pittsburgh, PA. Given his struggles with drugs, drinking and fighting, all part and parcel of growing up in a tough neighborhood, this was the best suggestion his probation officer could come up with. David III admires his dad. "I want to be just like my dad. He's intelligent, nice, caring, and understanding. . . He teaches that you're not supposed to hate anybody." And his father is proud of him, too.[34]

This is hardly the predictable outcome of a story that got off to a bad start. The senior Moore started serving a 17-35 year sentence while his son was just an infant. But he became one of nearly 600 inmates at the

---

34. Jeff Peck. 2002. "Restoring Incarcerated Fathers to their Children," in Prison Fellowship Ministries [online]. Merrifield, VA: Prison Fellowship Ministries, 2002 [cited August 8, 2002]. ‹http://www.prisonfellowship.org/PrisonFellowship/ChannelRoot/Home/Restoring+Incarcerated+Fathers+to+their+Children.htm›

facility who have participated in Long-Distance Dads (LDD), founded by Dr. Randell Turner, a program designed to prepare incarcerated fathers to shoulder their responsibilities to their children.

Chuck Colson has observed, "As the incidence of father absence grows, community disintegration and crime — especially youth crime — will continue to grow."[35] According to a 1999 study, the absence of a father is related to 63% of youth suicides, 90% of all homeless and runaway youths, 71% percent of high school dropouts, 70% of youths in state institutions, 75% of adolescent patients in substance abuse centers, and 80% of rapists who are motivated by displaced anger/rage. The Child Welfare League of America reports that children who have been abused and neglected are 67 times more likely than other children to be arrested between the ages of nine and twelve. And these kids are typically found in fatherless homes.

Thanks to several new programs, like LDD, prison psychologists, volunteers and corrections staff are trying out new approaches to bring a positive outcome. These programs help inmates who desire to improve themselves by teaching emotional management skills and other attributes that will make them better parents, and better citizens over all. And now, they and their children are spending more quality time "together" — even if it's just by phone or letter. "At least now I can talk to my kids about crime, what not to do, what was wrong with me, who's not so good to hang out with. I feel I play a role in their lives," Dennis J. explains. "They listen to me. They feel they have a dad, like other kids. And then, they don't feel quite so different, either."

LDD doesn't end with the finality of a prison sentence. Prior to "going home," fathers must complete specific schooling designed to strengthen parenting skills. A recently released graduate of LDD gained custody of his three boys (by three mothers) and, gathering them up from foster homes, has them all together for the first time, for example.

---

35. 1999 Study Internet Edition. "Parents in Prison," 2001.

LDD programs are being implemented in 26 penitentiaries so far, but has its strongest base in Pennsylvania. In the past two years, news of the program and its effects on inmates and their families is spreading. And where hope exists, there will be change.

Curtis Morrow and his daughter are now living together after his release from prison. Curtis, born to a crack-addicted mother with no maternal instincts, was raised by his grandparents in Erie after a few years of foster care. His father — married man — lived in Detroit with a good paying job as an assemblyman at GM. "Deep inside I longed to have that relationship, just to have a dad," Curtis sighted. Instead, he followed the predicted route of drugs followed by prison time. Just prior to his federal conviction for distribution, Curtis became a father, himself.

During parole, officials set a condition for reclaiming his daughter, who was in the foster care system: mandatory completion of LDD. He joined the program and took to it so wholeheartedly that he became a key player in the peer-led counseling sessions. He has his daughter back, now, and he has a good job. He still attends parenting sessions, and helps out other ex-criminals who need a lift and a babysitter so they can attend, themselves.

From 4-H to Mommy and Me classes, there is one union can't be blocked, even by cement slabs: parent — child relations. There is a passion to parent, which for many people seems to go on even when passions for the self have long since been lost. This hardwired desire to care for one's children holds the potential of rehabilitating behavior that could keep the next generation of children out of prison and reduce recidivism, child poverty, teen pregnancy and youth violence.

A FINAL ANALYSIS

We have looked at individual cases where restorative justice programs have been successful, and we have looked at communities who have reaped the benefits. As this enlightened methodology spreads across the states, we can begin to look forward to a new social awareness and, more important, a new judicial standard.

America lives with a criminal justice system in a chronic state of crisis. We are fearful and judgmental and angry. Many who work within the system are desensitized, forgetting that inmates are humans who need certain rights — rights to see their children, to have parole hearings, to educate themselves. But the criminal justice policy as a whole is mired in inertia, even when we have systematic information that suggests improvements can be made. The economic and social costs of current policy are not sustainable over long periods. Victims are often re-victimized by this "non-process." Looking toward the future, conservatives as well as liberals can only hope that a viable alternative is found. And it seems that restorative justice is viable, indeed.

There may not be a single blueprint to chart the journey toward building community support; nevertheless, these efforts need to be guided by a clear set of principles, and a specific strategy has to be implemented so that standards are maintained . . . only then, can we find a long-lasting solution to our criminal justice havoc.

Restorative justice is based on principles; it is also a way of thinking about how we respond to the problem of crime, criminals, victims and community. The methodology demands a redefinition of crime as injury to the victim and community, rather than as effrontery to the power of the state. The primary purpose of justice in the restorative model is to repair the harm done by the crime, to whatever degree possible.

The victim is not asked to be involved in order to force him or her to relive a vicious encounter, but rather to provide a perspective that is essential to the process of defining the harm in question. And then, identifying how that harm might be repaired. Restoring the victim means engaging the community as a resource for reconciliation of victims and offenders, and as a resource for monitoring and enforcing community standards of behavior. Restorative justice refuses to take sides: it merely embraces values.

Restorative justice also demands a change in the way the correctional institutions view inmates. Efforts by a corrections agency to stimulate change toward the restorative paradigm must of necessity present particular challenges. The framework calls for the inclusion of all stakeholders — so that the design and implementation of local justice practices may best befit its own community/ social structure. While the corrections agencies must work to their own guidelines, they should also be open to new ideologies introduced by individuals participating in the creation of restorative justice.

The irony is that any agency promoting change must model the values of restorative justice in its process by providing vision and encouragement to stakeholders while avoiding directives — yet there is an inherent tension between the traditionalists' need for details, in order to understand the framework's function, and the need for the leading agency to leave the details of implementation to be worked out during the participatory process.

The question of "how?" can be turned back to the participants, asking them to utilize the principles and identify practices, which fit the principles. The result over time can then be the illustration of multiple examples of restorative justice in practice, breathing life into the concept.

Restorative justice asks for a larger shift in our social institutions, from power-based structures and practices to relations-based structures and practices. Through the inmate populations (and their families and communities) who have benefited from such opportunity, through agencies who have upheld such standards, there is a growing inclination toward the miraculous success of a peace-making theory in practice: Restorative Justice.

We are locked in a desperate circle: Offender + Victim = Cycle. Restorative Justice offers an alternative that we desperately need. This new focus offers hope; hope for truly reaching peace, and truly finding answers to our conflicts, both internal and, of course, external. And then, the monstrous cycle can finally be broken.

GLOSSARY OF RESTORATIVE JUSTICE TERMINOLOGY FROM THE FRESNO COUNTY RESTORATIVE JUSTICE FRAMEWORK[36]

ACCOUNTABILTY

Genuine accountability includes an opportunity to understand the human consequences of one's actions, to face up to what one has done and to whom one has done it. Accountability also involves taking responsibility for the results of one's behavior (ownership in the outcome). As long as consequences are decided for offenders, accountability will not involve responsibility. Accountability empowers and encourages responsibility and takes seriously all three levels of need and obligation: victim, community and offender.

COMMUNITY

Who is the community in any given conflict will depend upon a number of factors, including the level of harm inflicted, the relationship of the disputants and the aggregation represented. There are many different levels of community, as there are different levels of disputes and conflicts. Each victim, disputant,

---

36.With thanks to the Fresno Pacific University Center for Peacemaking and Conflict Studies.
2002. "Fresno County Restorative Justice Framework," Services of the Restorative Justice Project of FPU [online]. Fresno, CA: Fresno Pacific University, February 2001 [cited August 1, 2002]. Available at <http://www.fresno.edu/pacs/docs/rjframe0201.pdf>.

offender may be members of several communities — family, friends, neighborhoods, schools, businesses, congregations and community organizations.

COMMUNITY JUSTICE

Community justice means that the community has the first responsibility to maintain peace. This means a transfer of authority to the community from political and governmental agencies. Government agencies provide support and back-up to the community justice processes, but do not dominate them. Community justice is a subset of the larger restorative justice ideas.

CONFLICTS, DISPUTES AND CRIMES

Conflicts, disputes and injustices occur when rights are threatened or violated, laws are transgressed or when people perceive that their objectives, hopes or aspirations are being blocked or removed by the acts of another. A crime is an offense specially designated by the common law or the legislature.

CONSEQUENCE

Consequences flow from conflicts, disputes, offenses, misbehaviors and crimes. The party's choice of cooperative processes leads to certain consequences. Restorative justice recognizes that some participants will be at times, non-cooperative and unwilling to participate in restorative processes. In these circumstances, the uncooperative party should be clearly aware of the consequences of non-cooperation. In the event a coercive process is required, coercion should be implemented in reasonable and respectful ways with the goal of achieving a restorative result. By restorative results, we mean that victims, offenders, or disputants are integrated or reintegrated into the community. Reconciliation is allowed to occur, and needs and obligations are met.

COVENANT JUSTICE

The belief in covenant justice, arising from the Jewish Pentateuch and the Christian Old Testament, states that God had made a covenant with people implying a reciprocal responsibility and commitment. This covenant created the basis for a new society that would work towards *shalom* (living in right relationships with God and one another). Similar expressions of right relationships among people are expressed in the sacred writings of Hinduism, Buddhism, Sikhism and Islam. Covenant justice makes things right, to build *shalom* by acting on behalf of those in need, to be concerned with needs, not merit. Justice is tested by the outcome, and process, for corrective discipline occurs in a content of constructive community accompanied by a renewal of the covenant. Retribution is subordinate to *shalom*, which tempers and limits retributive justice.

CRIME

Crime is primarily an offense against human relationships and secondarily a violation of penal law.

HEALING

Disputants in conflicts, disputes and offenses often need to be healed. Healing requires opportunities for forgiveness, confession, repentance and reconciliation. The healing process includes empowerment, truth telling, answers to questions, restoring equity, and creating constructive future intentions.

MEDIATION — ARBRITRATION — TRIAL

Mediation is a dispute-resolution process in which the disputants bring in a fair third party to assist tin finding resolution. The third party does not make the decision. Mediation may be facilitative or directive, adversarial or cooperative. The parties have the power to resolve the dispute, which occurs only when they're in unanimous assent.

Arbitration is a private judicial proceeding in which the disputants bring in a third party, usually neutral, to decide the dispute based on evidence presented. Formal rules of evidence and procedure may not apply. The parties have no power to decide the dispute; they invest all power in decision making to the third party. Arbitration may be adversarial or cooperative.

Trial is a public judicial proceeding in which the disputants present their case to a judge or jury for a decision based on formal rules of evidence and rules of procedure. Professionals represent parties. The parties have no power to decide the dispute; they invest all power in decision making to the judge or jury and delegate substantial authority to the professional in matters concerning strategy and tactics. Trial is always adversarial, never cooperative.

OFFENDER

An Offender is a person who causes injury to another or who causes resentful displeasure in another. The *primary offender* is the individual principally responsible for the harm. The *secondary offenders* are those whose behavior creates the conditions that contribute to conflicts, disputes, crime or violence.

PRIMARY DISPUTE RESOLUTON (PDR)

Primary dispute resolution refers to those dispute resolution processes utilized before adversary processes are engaged. PDR is distinguished from *Alternative Dispute Resolution* in that ADR implies processes that are alternatives to arbitration or trial, thus giving adversary processes primacy in a dispute resolution system. In contrast, PDR gives cooperative dispute resolution processes primacy. Adversary processes, such as arbitration or trial, should be considered a back-up for the parties when they have failed to reach a cooperative agreement to resolve the conflict. There are civil and criminal cases which require that a trial take precedence over PDR. Even these trials should be conducted under restorative justice principles.

RECONCLIATION

Reconciliation is the settlement of a conflict, dispute or offense that includes improving friendly relations with someone after an estrangement. Reconciliation is a primary focus of restorative justice.

REINTEGRATION AND INTEGRATION

The process of reintegration and integration concerns those persons who have been damaged and estranged through disputes, misbehaviors, and crimes; and the acceptance of them back into the community.

REMEDIES

Remedies consist of four classes of relief available at law. Those classes include substitutionary remedies (compensation for what was lost and measured by the value of the thing lost), equitable remedies (coercive orders), declaratory remedies (declaration of rights and obligations under

Restorative Justice

instruments or statutes), and restitutionary remedies (preventing unjust enrichment, measured by the value of the benefit conferred). Restorative justice remedies are broader than classical legal remedies and are therefore preferred for resolving conflicts, disputes and offenses.

RESTORATIVE DISCIPLINE

Restorative Discipline is restorative justice when applied as school and at home. Restorative Discipline is a way of responding to conflict and misbehavior that makes things as right as possible for all who were impacted. Restorative Discipline includes recognizing the conflict or harm, repairing the damage (physical and relational) as much as possible and creating plans and/or agreements that will prevent the same thing from happening again. Restorative Discipline includes programs, processes, and procedures that are guided by restorative justice principles. (See Chapter two, Principles)

RETRIBUTIVE JUSTICE (RETRIBUTIVE DISCIPLINE)

Retributive justice (or discipline) is a way of responding to conflict, misbehavior, and crime that assumes that things are made as right as possible by administering pain to persons who have violated rules or laws. Retributive justice is guided by policies and procedure intended to limit and determine the appropriate amount of pain administered by those in charge.

VICTIM

A Victim is a person who suffers from a destructive or injurious action or agency. The *primary victim* in the one most impacted by the offense. The *secondary victims* include others impacted by the crime. These secondary victims may include family members, friends, criminal justice officials, community, etc.